New Challenges in Immigration Theory

T0347531

As far as immigration theory is concerned, the attempt to reconcile concern for all persons with the reality of state boundaries and exclusionary policies has proved difficult within the limits of normative liberal political philosophy. However, the *realpolitik* of migration in today's environment forces a major paradigm shift. We must move beyond standard debates between those who argue for more open borders and those who argue for more closed borders. This book aims to show that a realistic utopia of political theory of immigration is possible, but argues that to do so we must focus on expanding the boundaries of what are familiar normative positions in political theory. Theorists must better inform themselves of the concrete challenges facing migration policies: statelessness, brain drain, migrant rights, asylum policies, migrant detention practices, climate refugees, etc. We must ask: *what is the best we can and ought to wish for* in the face of these difficult migration challenges.

Blake, Carens, and Cole offer pieces that outline the major normative questions in the political theory of immigration. The positions these scholars outline are challenged by the pieces contributed by Lister, Ottonelli, Torresi, Sager, and Silverman. These latter pieces force the reformulation of the central positions in normative political theory of immigration.

This book was originally published as a special issue of the *Critical Review of International Social and Political Philosophy.*

Crispino E.G. Akakpo is currently a Doctoral Researcher at the Institute of Philosophy, University of Leuven, Belgium, where he works on political philosophy and the philosophy of law. He aims to develop criteria for just migration policies by exploring the tension between moral universalism and state-based exclusion.

Patti T. Lenard is Assistant Professor of Applied Ethics at the Graduate School of Public and International Affairs at the University of Ottawa, Canada. Her first book, *Trust, Democracy and Multicultural Challenges* (2012), focused on the challenges posed by diversity, largely caused by immigration, in domestic states. Her current research focuses on the normative questions that arise as people cross borders, and the reasons that states provide to justify admitting and excluding migrants.

New Challenges in Immigration Theory

Edited by
**Crispino E.G. Akakpo and
Patti T. Lenard**

Routledge
Taylor & Francis Group

LONDON AND NEW YORK

First published 2015
by Routledge

2 Park Square, Milton Park, Abingdon, Oxon OX14 4RN
711 Third Avenue, New York, NY 10017, USA

Routledge is an imprint of the Taylor & Francis Group, an informa business

First issued in paperback 2017

British Library Cataloguing in Publication Data
A catalogue record for this book is available from the British Library

ISBN 13: 978-1-138-85641-7 (hbk)
ISBN 13: 978-1-138-05756-2 (pbk)

Typeset in Times New Roman
by RefineCatch Limited, Bungay, Suffolk

Publisher's Note
The publisher accepts responsibility for any inconsistencies that may have
arisen during the conversion of this book from journal articles to book chapters,
namely the possible inclusion of journal terminology.

Disclaimer
Every effort has been made to contact copyright holders for their permission to
reprint material in this book. The publishers would be grateful to hear from any
copyright holder who is not here acknowledged and will undertake to rectify
any errors or omissions in future editions of this book.

Contents

Citation Information

The chapters in this book were originally published in the *Critical Review of International Social and Political Philosophy*, volume 17, issue 5 (July–December 2014). When citing this material, please use the original page numbering for each article, as follows:

Chapter 1
New challenges in immigration theory: an overview
Crispino E.G. Akakpo and Patti T. Lenard
Critical Review of International Social and Political Philosophy, volume 17, issue 5 (July–December 2014) pp. 493–502

Chapter 2
Beyond reason: the philosophy and politics of immigration
Phillip Cole
Critical Review of International Social and Political Philosophy, volume 17, issue 5 (July–December 2014) pp. 503–520

Chapter 3
The right to exclude
Michael Blake
Critical Review of International Social and Political Philosophy, volume 17, issue 5 (July–December 2014) pp. 521–537

Chapter 4
An overview of the ethics of immigration
Joseph H. Carens
Critical Review of International Social and Political Philosophy, volume 17, issue 5 (July–December 2014) pp. 538–559

Chapter 5

Reframing the brain drain
Alex Sager
Critical Review of International Social and Political Philosophy, volume 17, issue 5 (July–December 2014) pp. 560–579

Chapter 6

Temporary migration projects and voting rights
Valeria Ottonelli and Tiziana Torresi
Critical Review of International Social and Political Philosophy, volume 17, issue 5 (July–December 2014) pp. 580–599

Chapter 7

Detaining immigrants and asylum seekers: a normative introduction
Stephanie J. Silverman
Critical Review of International Social and Political Philosophy, volume 17, issue 5 (July–December 2014) pp. 600–617

Chapter 8

Climate change refugees
Matthew Lister
Critical Review of International Social and Political Philosophy, volume 17, issue 5 (July–December 2014) pp. 618–634

Please direct any queries you may have about the citations to
clsuk.permissions@cengage.com

Notes on Contributors

Crispino E.G. Akakpo is a DBOF Doctoral Fellow at the Institute of Philosophy, Catholic University of Leuven, Belgium. He is examining the tension between moral universalism and state-based exclusion in order to develop the normative grounds for a just migration policy. His research interests (in political philosophy and philosophy of law) include Immigration, Justice, Liberty, Sovereignty, Democracy, Constitutionalism, Natural Law, and Principles of Legality.

Michael Blake is Professor of Philosophy and Public Affairs at the University of Washington, Seattle, USA. He works on international justice and on the morality of immigration. He is currently finishing a book on the ethics of the brain drain, written as a debate with Gillian Brock.

Joseph H. Carens is a Professor of Political Science at the University of Toronto, Canada. His research focuses on questions about justice, equality, and freedom in democratic communities. He is particularly interested in the normative issues raised by the movement of people across state borders and by ethnic and cultural diversity in all its forms.

Phillip Cole is a Visiting Professor of Applied Philosophy with the Social Ethics Research Group, University of South Wales, Newport, UK, and a Senior Lecturer in Politics and International Development at the University of West of England, Bristol, UK. His research interests are human rights and international migration, the right to healthcare, and the connections between political theory and critical activism. His most recent book is co-written with Christopher Wellman, and is titled *Debating the Ethics of Immigration: Is there a Right to Exclude?* (2011).

Patti T. Lenard is Assistant Professor of Ethics in the Graduate School of Public and International Affairs at the University of Ottawa, Canada. She is the author of *Trust, Democracy and Multicultural Challenges* (2012), and her work has been published in a range of journals, including *Political Studies, Politics, Journal of Moral Philosophy*, and *Contemporary Political Theory*. She is the co-editor, with Christine Straehle, of *Health Inequalities and Global Justice*, as well as *Legislated Inequality: Temporary Labour Migration in Canada*. Her current research focuses on the moral questions raised by migration across borders, as well as on multiculturalism, trust and social cohesion, and democratic theory more generally.

Matthew Lister is a Visiting Assistant Professor in the Department of Legal Studies and Business Ethics at the Wharton School of Business, University of Pennsylvania. He has taught at the University of Pennsylvania Law School, the University of Denver, Sturm College of Law, and Villanova Law School. He works on immigration law and policy, international law more generally, jurisprudence, and political philosophy, including its history.

Valeria Ottonelli is Lecturer at the Department of Philosophy, University of Genoa, Italy. She works on the issue of immigration and the right to freedom of movement between states, and on the normative theory of democracy, with particular regard to the contrast between proceduralism and instrumentalism.

Alex Sager is an Assistant Professor of Philosophy and University Studies at Portland State University, Portland, OR, USA. His main research program is in applied political philosophy on topics surrounding migration.

Stephanie J. Silverman is a Research Associate at the Refugee Research Network, Centre for Refugee Studies and Course Coordinator, Community Research Partnerships in Ethics, Trinity College, University of Toronto. Her research has been published in *Forced Migration Review*, *Politics & Policy*, *Population, Space and Place*, and *Refuge: Canada's Journal on Forced Migration*, and her co-edited book on the global spread of immigration detention and its impact on protection for asylum seekers will be published by Routledge in May 2015.

Tiziana Torresi is Lecturer in International Politics at the University of Adelaide, Australia. Her research focuses on the normative theory of migration. She works on temporary migration, normative critiques of emerging patterns of international migration governance, and migration and political representation.

New challenges in immigration theory: an overview

Crispino E.G. Akakpo[a] and Patti T. Lenard[b]

[a]Institute of Philosophy, KU Leuven, Leuven, Belgium; [b]Graduate School of Public and International Affairs, University of Ottawa, Ottawa, Canada

Normative political theory over recent decades has focused mainly on what *ought* to be done as far as migration policies are concerned. It faces a basic challenge, which stems from two competing, yet equally fundamental, ideals underpinning liberal democratic societies: a commitment to moral universalism and the exclusionary requirement of democracy. The objective of this special issue, 'New Challenges in Immigration Theory', is to provide a conceptual overview of (some) immigration theories and to highlight the challenges new streams of immigration pose for normative (political) theory and liberal democratic practice. The issue will consider how to reconcile state-based exclusion with a commitment to equal moral concern for all persons, by focusing on the non-standard immigration questions that have so far been 'neglected' by normative political theory. In line with this objective, the issue will discuss some of the inadequacies of the dominant political theories of immigration and show how such theories can be expanded to take account of new migration challenges such as brain drain, climate migration, detention of irregular migrants and asylum seekers, rights of labour migrants, transnational networks of movement, and so on.

Introduction

Normative political theory of immigration had its birth in a response to John Rawls' proposal that, to identify the best principles of domestic justice, we should willingly accept the 'considerable abstraction' that societies are closed, and thus offer their citizens a 'more or less complete and self-sufficient scheme of cooperation, making room within itself for all the necessary activities of life, from birth to death' (Rawls 1993, p. 18). The response questioned two assumptions in this statement: that entering and exiting societies transpired only by birth and death and that a complete life can necessarily easily and satisfyingly be lived within the confines of one state. In fact, it was, and is, increasingly the case that people enter societies via migration and that more and more people spend portions of their lives living outside of their state of citizenship. These observations served to highlight a tension in liberal democratic theory: whereas liberal political philosophy is founded on a commitment to the moral equality of persons, immigration challenges this commitment by highlighting that the right of states to choose their members treats others unequally in some key respects. Attempts to reconcile the liberal universal concern for all persons with the reality of state boundaries and their exclusionary policies continue to prove difficult within the limits of liberal political theory.

This special issue, 'New Challenges in Immigration Theory', provides a conceptual overview of the central debates in immigration and then goes on to highlight the challenges that new streams of immigration pose for normative (political) theory and liberal democratic practice. In so doing, the issue will contribute to ongoing attempts to reconcile state-based exclusion with a commitment to equal moral concern for all persons. By focusing on the non-standard immigration questions that have so far been neglected by normative political theory, the contributions highlight some of the weaknesses of the dominant political theories of immigration, and suggest some strategies we can deploy to expand the normative boundaries in order to account for these new migration challenges, which range from those posed by high- and low-skilled labour migration to those posed by climate migration and border control strategies. Michael Blake and Phillip Cole outline the major normative questions in the political theory of immigration. The normative positions these scholars outline are challenged by the articles contributed by Alexander Sager, Joseph Carens, Valeria Ottonelli and Tiziana Torresi, Stephanie Silverman and Mathew Lister. These latter articles aim to force the reformulation of the central positions in normative political theory of immigration. Their contributions highlight that offering a persuasive theory of immigration demands that political theorists work very hard to inform themselves of the concrete challenges facing all three parties to immigration: migrants, sending states and receiving states.

Framing the debate

So-called open border theorists challenge the deeply embedded assumptions of liberal democratic theory, which ignored, as Rawls did, that membership in a political society itself is a source of moral, and increasingly also, political controversy. Led by Carens' (1987) seminal defence of open borders, many scholars became preoccupied by an ignored, but glaring tension in liberal democratic theory; between two competing, yet equally fundamental ideals underpinning liberal democratic societies: a commitment to moral universalism and the apparent, and always assumed without justification, exclusionary requirement of democracy. An open borders position stems from focusing on the perspective of the migrant, i.e. to privilege her right to cross borders except in exceptional circumstances, and to adopt a position of wariness towards claims that more migration is unfeasible (Kukathas 2005).

Fundamentally, says Phillip Cole in the introductory piece to this special issue, it is not possible to reconcile coercive borders with a commitment to equality; here and elsewhere, Cole (2000, 2006) rejects attempts like Blake's to argue for the moral relevance of borders, even in a world that is just along all other dimensions. Cole says, 'immigration controls represent the failure of liberal political theory'. It is, in particular, a mistake to imbue the borders that divide states with moral relevance – Cole rejects the claim that it is possible to defend political borders, in spite of their historically arbitrary placement; they cannot, as Michael Blake claims in his contribution to the special issue, justify a distinction in the rights possessed by those on one or the other side of state borders. Their very *arbitrariness* makes them indefensible, and defending them highlights the incoherence of attempting to justify views according to which citizens can enjoy better or worse life prospects in virtue of their relative location with respect to an arbitrarily erected border.

The response to this challenge, or to the demand that liberal democracy defend its exclusionary assumptions, is multifold. For some, it seems transparently obvious that one feature of democratic self-determination is the right to have full or nearly full control over the membership of a population (Simmons 2001); it is integral to our understanding of sovereignty that membership is at the discretion of the already existing members. For others, the defences rest on protecting the social cohesion on which democratic practice depends; social cohesion is a fragile and essential democratic resource, and since immigrants, in some cases, can threaten social cohesion, and since democratic states are best able to judge when this is a threat, democratic states are justified in controlling their membership (Miller 2005). And for others still, the exclusionary tendencies are defended for their contributions to protecting access to social justice policies for members. These social justice policies – those that are defended by egalitarian political theorists – are so valuable that, if it is possible that immigration threatens them, the democratic community is justified in excluding by reference to a critically important good, i.e. the importance of fair distribution of material resources within a democratic state. Another component of this argument worries, with some justification, that the social cohesion that underpins a commitment to redistributive policies can be threatened by an influx of immigrants who remain at the margin of society.

In response to Cole's complaint, and others like it, Michael Blake offers an attempt to justify the state's right to exclude. At the heart of Blake's jurisdictional justification for exclusion are the relationships that bind members of an already existing political state, and the obligations to which these relationships give rise. This justification for exclusion, says Blake, stems from a commitment to avoid imposing obligations on individuals – we have, he argues, at least a limited right to protect ourselves from incurring unwanted obligations. We can do this by examining the right to exit, which is in part protected because no government can compel its citizens to remain, for the reason that doing so forces them into relations they prefer to sever. Any migrant's demand to enter can, similarly, be resisted by citing the desire of the excluding state to be protected from forming unwanted relations and the attendant obligations. The advantage of his approach is, it avoids resting on controversial cultural defences of the right to exclude; the good of community is a good worth preserving, Blake acknowledges, but not one that is so significant as to justify complete exclusion as some sometimes are thought to suggest (Walzer 1983).

Cole and Blake's views serve as bookends of a sort, delineating a strong case for the right to move as well as a strong case for the right of states to exclude. Having identified the parameters of the debate between open and closed border advocates, the remaining contributions to this issue focus on the specific migration patterns to which these theories might apply. The contributors thus aim to encourage a discussion between the framework offered by the political theory of migration and these new and difficult migration challenges.

In particular, the contributions to this special issue raise specific challenges to immigration theory by focusing on discrete migratory streams, rather than migration as a whole. They show us that the normative questions raised by each of these streams are distinct and that it is worth treating them independently. Together, they serve to challenge our basic understanding of the phenomenon of migration itself, forcing us to think more seriously about three key elements of the migratory experience, including: (1) when migration serves and when it undermines global redistributive justice, (2) the (moral and practical) significance of the timing of migratory decisions and (3) the locus of coercion in the migration experience.

Rethinking the global distributive justice challenge to immigration control

When Carens' seminal article appeared, among the most compelling images was that of poor Haitians, in leaky boats, approaching the American shore, asking for admission. Carens had his readers envision the justification we might legitimately offer these poor migrants, for hoarding our goods to ourselves, and moreover, for pointing guns at them to prevent them from entering and thus from sharing these goods. This image helped to fuel his claim that the global state structure, which protects nation-state borders alongside the right of these nation-states to make admission and exclusion decisions with near impunity, was best understood as an analogy to feudal times: 'citizenship in Western liberal democracies is the modern equivalent of feudal privilege – an inherited status that greatly enhances one's life chances' (Carens 1987, p. 252). His readers were intended to take away this lesson: in a world riddled with inequalities, the justifications for excluding the poor from wealthy states carry little weight. Rather, the right to migrate across borders ought, under these profoundly unequal conditions, to be protected from wealthy states' desire to restrict entry, even where the attempt to restrict entry is defended for its contribution to protecting egalitarian resource distribution in the domestic state. For at least some thinkers, where the welfare state is at risk as a result of an influx of migrants, so much the worse for the welfare state (Kukathas 2005). The wealth disparities between the poorest and wealthiest of citizens may have lessened slightly since Carens' proposal to think of migration as (at least) a second-best mechanism by which to enable at least some redistribution of wealth, but remedying global poverty remains a profound and seemingly intractable challenge. Thus, although Blake asks what we learn about the right to exclude from considering a more or less equal world, several of the contributions take for granted the wealth inequalities that propel and constrain migration in the current global environment, and consider how we should treat the right to migrate within this context. They avoid the philosophically consistent, but practically unhelpful, proposal that wealthy states can in principle avoid admitting poor migrants, since after all they could discharge their duties to those who are less well-off by, for example, 'exporting' political or economic justice.[1]

The setting for Alex Sager's assessment of the normative challenges allegedly posed by the 'brain drain', as well as Tiziana Torresi and Valeria Ottonelli's evaluation of the goals of temporary labour migrants, is the international order that prioritizes, and indeed upholds, national institutions, and thereby, the right to exclude. This international order must be understood as framing migratory decisions, since it in effect is responsible for generating and sustaining migration policies that disadvantage those who are poorest and most vulnerable. It is in that context that we must evaluate the alleged benefits and burdens of brain drain, the 'loss' of skilled workers across a range of sectors from developing states, who migrate to developed states in pursuit of better economic opportunities and working conditions. The standard objection is that brain drain is an insidious way in which developing nations subsidize developed nations, who enjoy the benefits of migrants' skills without having to shoulder the costs of producing skilled citizens. But, says Sager, the evidence to support the claim that the exodus of skilled migrants has a negative distributional effect is weak to non-existent; rather, he says, there is considerable evidence to the contrary, which suggests it has neutral and perhaps even positive distributional consequences. In light of this evidence, Sager argues, the claim that exit restrictions can legitimately be imposed on skilled migrants loses much of its force. Even those that are restricted in time – those that require, for example, that migrants labour in their field of study to 'repay' the state for the cost of their education – cannot be adequately justified. Fundamentally, they serve simply to prevent migrants from migrating at the moment they prefer, and thus hamper their freedom to make choices about how their lives will proceed.

Migration in time

Political theory of immigration has tended to treat migration as a single decision, which occurs at a single moment in time. We are led to imagine the simple situation, of a migrant who arrives at the border, asking to be admitted – representatives of the political community wait there, to adjudicate the case, and admit or exclude. But several of the pieces in this special issue question this understanding of migratory decision-making. Not only are migration decisions made in non-discrete moments in time, but rather over a period of time, it is also the case that the actions of the receiving states have significant effects on the 'time dimension' of migration, in particular of identifying the moment at which migrants can be said to have, effectively, migrated.

Joseph Carens offers a clear account of the role that time should play in extending citizenship status to migrants. He argues that the longer the stay of migrants (legal or illegal), the stronger the claim to remain becomes. This well-known argument, explored in our issue in relation to a range of migrant categories, emphasizes that the moral claims imposed simply by the passage of time must be taken seriously. Over time, migrants form relations with others around them, often with citizens and they form expectations about how their lives will proceed. As a result, injustice is done to migrants by forcing them into retaining an irregular status over an extended period or by requiring that they return after a lengthy stay. Avoiding this injustice demands extending them citizenship, or at least the right to apply for citizenship in time. The democratic claim – that those who reside in a given territory, and whose laws have a significant impact on their lives are morally entitled to have a say in what those laws are – buttresses this conclusion. Where states rely on migrants in their economy, and where these migrants are either labouring under 'irregular' or temporary conditions, they are in effect creating a second class of citizens who remain marginalized. Carens' argument concludes, therefore, that any mechanism that does not place these migrants on the path to citizenship is unjust. Applied to temporary labour migrants, this framework tells us that emphasizing the length of time migrants spend residing in a host state reveals the injustice of many of the laws that regulate the lives of temporary labour migrants. In many states, these migrants are prevented, by law, from attaining citizenship and in most states, the constraints placed on them make it clear that they are to consider their sending state their home (Lenard and Straehle 2012).

However, Tiziana Torresi and Valeria Ottonelli challenge the proposal that the right thing to do, in the face of injustices that temporary labour migrants so often face, is to extend them citizenship rights.[2] Instead, they reason that granting full political rights, including the right to political participation, poorly serves the class of migrants who do not seek to become full members of their host societies but plan to return to their home countries. Since these migrants intend to migrate on a temporary basis only, with the sole aim of bettering their economic prospects in their home state, granting them citizenship rights might actually infringe on their autonomy, i.e. their ability to choose and revise their life plans. Thus, such migrants will be forced to partake in a project that negates their basic interests and rational goals since citizenship requires engagement with the full repertoire of democratic requirements and burdens. Trade unions and migrant labour organizations, Torresi and Ottonelli assert,

6

can better advance the interests of these migrants. The idea is that the political voices of trade unions stand a better chance of influencing policies bearing on labour issues than that of migrants even if they are granted the right of political participation. This contribution questions the general liberal and democratic intuition that subjects of coercive laws must be its authors, a principle on which Carens relies to justify his call for setting all migrants on the path to citizenship.

Carens' proposal is also challenged by Silverman's focus on the ethics governing the expanding use of detention facilities in western democratic states. Carens would surely object to the use of detention – in particular, in light of the evidence Silverman cites that other, less intrusive, mechanisms keep track of immigrants just as effectively. Not only is it often an unjustified restriction on a whole host of freedoms that liberal democratic states value, it is often deployed in arbitrary, humiliating, ways. Yet, the very justification for detaining migrants in centres – that it prevents the absconding of migrants – forces us to reconsider the way in which we understand the passing of time, as generating at least a moral case for citizenship. For example, if migrants are detained for extended periods of time in a detention centre, not all of the reasons for imbuing time spent in a host state as generating the right to citizenship apply. Although Carens at no point argues that the sole *reason* for time's moral relevance is that individuals form meaningful relations with others in the community, intuitively his argument is attractive for the ways in which we believe that the relations formed over time do in fact have significant weight. At least part of the harm of forced removal is the breaking of relations between migrants and those in their community: the well-publicized attempts, for example, to prevent the deportation of migrants focus squarely on the relations they have formed with the community that has become their home (Gibney 2008). Some states even acknowledge the weight of these relations formally – on the list of when migrants facing deportation, in Germany, can be granted leave to stay, is when they cohabitate with German citizens, for example. For now, the point is simply to observe that the use of detention centres as a mechanism for preventing the absconding of migrants also prevents them from generating the relationships that give rise to the relations that, over time, matter from the perspective of granting, or not, rights of citizenship to long-term residents.

Coercion and voluntariness

The act of detaining migrants highlights the coercive nature of borders, and in particular, of border *control*. The question of whether borders themselves, enforced as they are by a range of mechanisms, are coercive has recently occupied attention of migration theorists. For some, their very existence exerts coercion on those who cannot, or are unlikely to be, admitted: drawing on the resources provided by democratic theory, Abizadeh (2008) has argued that *all* those who are coerced by a given political decision are entitled to justification.

If that is right, he tells us, then those who find themselves excluded by borders are themselves entitled to justification. We might not agree – for example, Miller (2010) does not – that the effect of borders is *coercive,* by which he means that they do not force certain choices on us; thus, the effect of being denied the right to cross them is not such as to inflict significant hardship.

The contributions to this issue complicate or blur the line between coerced and voluntary migration. Historically, the line demarcating voluntary from coerced migration has been over-simplified. It is readily agreed states are required to admit genuine refugees, i.e. those who are coerced into migrating, to flee war, genocide, persecution are so on; these migrants must be permitted, by international law, to exercise their right to exit and corresponding right to entry into a safe environment (Whelan 1981). Not all scholars limit their understanding of refugees to those escaping political violence; others observe that migration to escape poverty merits being treated, effectively, as forced migration as well. For example, Pogge (1997) suggests that the threat of political persecution and poverty are equally morally powerful reasons to migrate and to warrant a right to admission. Furthermore, says Mathew Lister, in his contribution to this special issue, the *logic* of the UN definition of a legitimate refugee can be relied upon to defend the right to admission of at least one category of climate migrants, those who are forced into crossing borders, as a result of a threat that is likely to be of indefinite duration, and where the specific threat is to the ability to live a decent life. Just as in the case of those already captured by the Geneva Convention's definition of a refugee, these climate migrants are forced to cross borders against their will.

What of migrants who are prevented by their home states from migrating? Historically, of course, where migrants are prevented from exercising their right to exit, their home states are subject to international condemnation. But the exit restrictions that occupy Sager are not thought, at first glance, to be objectionable. Sager, as we noted above, questions their most frequently cited rationale: the contribution that the migration of skilled workers makes to perpetuating inequality. If this rationale cannot be justified, neither can coercive attempts to retain skilled migrants. This debate, however, tells us that the simple understanding of the right to exit one's state, as a basic human right, must be made more complicated. Contemporary migration theory stands in need of an account of when, if ever, states can legitimately restrict exit, and when these restrictions are as coercive as borders are said to be.

Conclusion

Readers do not need this special issue to remind them that migration is a complex phenomenon, which in all of its varieties confronts our basic normative assumptions about political community, including what members of the community owe to each other and to others. Our modest objective has been to highlight the complexities of some specific forms of migration, with the hope that doing so will serve to underpin a more sophisticated political theory of migration.

Acknowledgements

We would like to thank all the authors for their contributions to this volume, Richard Bellamy and the referee from CRISPP for suggestions and comments.

Notes

1. The proposal is practically unhelpful since wealthy states are so unwilling to participate in adequate redistributive schemes across borders. As a result, proposals to avoid the claim that states are duty-bound to admit migrants, by suggesting they could alternatively devote resources to material redistribution, act more like a philosophical 'get out of jail free' card than they do a genuine proposal for improving the conditions of those who are least well-off.
2. As for example, is argued in Lenard (2012).

References

Abizadeh, A., 2008. Democratic theory and border coercion: no right to unilaterally control your own borders. *Political theory*, 36, 37–65.

Carens, J., 1987. Aliens and citizens: the case for open borders. *The review of politics*, 49, 251–273.

Cole, P., 2000. *Philosophies of exclusion: liberal political theory and immigration.* Edinburgh: Edinburgh University Press.

Cole, P., 2006. Towards a symmetrical world: migration and international law. *Ethics and economics*, 4, 1–7.

Gibney, M.J., 2008. Asylum and the expansion of deportation in the United Kingdom. *Government and opposition*, 43, 146–167.

Kukathas, C., 2005. The case for open migration. *In*: Andrew Cohen and Christopher Heath Wellman, eds. *Contemporary debates in applied ethics*. Oxford: Blackwell, 207–220.

Lenard, P.T., 2012. Why temporary labour migration is not a satisfactory alternative to permanent migration. *Journal of international political theory*, 8, 172–183.

Lenard, P.T. and Straehle, C., 2012. Temporary labour migration, global redistribution, and democratic justice. *Politics, philosophy & economics*, 11, 206–230.

Miller, D., 2005. Immigration: the case for limits. *In*: Andrew Cohen and Christopher Heath Wellman, eds. *Contemporary debates in applied ethics*. Oxford: Blackwell, 193–207.

Miller, D., 2010. Why immigration controls are not coercive: a reply to Arash Abizadeh. *Political theory*, 38, 111–120.

Pogge, T., 1997. Migration and poverty. *In*: Veit Bader, ed. *Citizenship and exclusion*. Basingstoke: MacMillan Press, 12–27.

Rawls, J., 1993. *Political liberalism*. New York: Columbia University Press.

Simmons, A.J., 2001. On the territorial rights of states. *Noûs*, 35, 300–326.

Walzer, M., 1983. *Spheres of justice: a defense of pluralism and equality*. New York: Basic Books.

Whelan, F.G., 1981. Citizenship and the right to leave. *The American political science review*, 75, 636–653.

Beyond reason: the philosophy and politics of immigration

Phillip Cole

Politics and International Relations, University of the West of England, Bristol, UK

In this paper, I critically address the role of arbitrary and contingent features in philosophical debates about migration. These features play a central role, and display the importance of 'unreason' in the debate and the limits of rational criticism. Certain elements of political thought have to be taken as given, as essential starting points or indispensable building blocks. As such, they cannot be exposed to rational criticism. Political arrangements such as national borders, nation-states and national identities constitute these building blocks, and justify coercive borders in order to sustain them. If we are to subject these arrangements to critical examination, then we move beyond the limits of liberal political philosophy. I examine theorists who take this kind of approach to the ethics of immigration: Michael Blake, Samuel Scheffler and David Miller. I argue that such approaches ask us to balance arbitrary and contingent features of the political world against the non-contingent moral equality of the migrant. If we are to recognize the migrant as an equal reason-giver in the moral contestation of borders, then we are compelled to theorize beyond these limits, and to theorize instead about a global community of equals, a post-national world made up of transnational belonging.

As I write this paper, the subject of immigration is at the forefront of public political debate in the United Kingdom, but it is a debate in which political philosophy plays little or no role. In a way, this is not surprising as philosophy is committed to the use of reason and evidence, but when it comes to public debates about immigration, reason and evidence fly out of the window. Immigrants are accused of being benefit tourists, of getting priority over 'natives' when it comes to housing and other social goods, undermining social cohesion or national unity, and increasing crime. But the evidence is that they do not perform such antisocial acts any more than the 'natives', and there is evidence that in many cases, they are less likely to perform these acts.[1] And yet the vast majority of people, when confronted by this evidence, simply do not believe it. In the words of Moe Szyslak: 'Immigants! I knew it was them! Even when it was the bears, I knew it was them' (*The Simpsons: Much ado about Apu*). This refusal to see the evidence is not confined to what we might consider far-right anti-immigrant groups, but includes a great deal of the political and intellectual public debate. Jonathan Portes comments on David Goodhart's recent contribution to that debate (Goodhart 2013, Portes 2013): 'Goodhart argues that low-skilled immigrants have taken jobs from unskilled natives, leaving them languishing on benefits, while high-skilled immigration reduces both the incentives and opportunities for ambitious and talented natives to move up the ladder'. But while many, including the political elite, accept this thesis, there is 'almost no evidence to support it' (Portes 2013, p. 7). Portes argues that Goodhart cannot escape his 'instinctive view that the political economy of immigration is a zero-sum game', even though 'both economic theory and the evidence say no such thing' (Portes 2013, p. 7). This 'instinctive view' is deeply embedded in the public sphere, and indeed sometimes intrudes into the academic sphere.

It is important for philosophers to consider this level of unreason, because it identifies the place where philosophy encounters the anti-theoretical, a border which reason is not permitted to cross. Here, we face the refusal to recognize the validity of relevant argument and evidence, and so we could describe this as an encounter with the irrational. It is this encounter with the irrational that makes it difficult for political philosophy to contribute to the public debate, and yet at the same time, it has a moral duty to do so. But what is the public role of philosophy in this encounter? If philosophers wish to enter the public sphere, then we have to consider how to engage with the anti-theoretical, possibly irrational, element of that sphere. To suppose, we can enter it by debating issues in the same way that we debate them in the 'philosophical' sphere is naïve, and probably unhelpful.[2]

I am not going to explore this challenge here.[3] Instead, I want to look at a subject related to it, and that is the *legitimate* role of unreason in the philosophical debate about the ethics of immigration. The vast majority of liberal political theorists believe that it is possible to offer a moral justification of coercive borders: that the state has the moral right to use its coercive powers to prevent migrants entering its territory or membership; and/or has the moral right to impose conditions upon those migrants who are granted permission to enter, over and above those conditions of membership imposed on those who are already residents/citizens – e.g. conditions of integration. The challenge these theorists face is in reconciling that right with the liberal commitment to the moral equality of persons. Coercive borders appear to violate that central ethical commitment. Michael Blake recognizes the importance of this challenge. He points out that: '... liberals are committed to some form of equal moral concern and respect for all who share common humanity. No person or group of persons is to be arbitrarily excluded from the reach of liberal justice'. But liberalism 'has been developed as a theory primarily within the context of the nation-state' (Blake 2005, p. 225). Within this context, the task has been to 'figure out what principles could justify political power' (Blake 2005, p. 225). If we cannot find a way to reconcile these two features of liberal political theory, then the power of exclusion from membership will remain just that – the exercise of power, not of right. I have argued elsewhere that in a morally non-arbitrary world, the only coherent and consistent position for liberal political theory to take is to argue for complete freedom of international movement. Immigration controls represent the moral failure of liberal political theory.[4]

But as well as meeting the challenge presented by the principle of moral equality, theorists who wish to justify coercive borders face a second challenge, one that is sometimes overlooked. Another characteristic element of liberal philosophy is what could be described as the rationality principle, the assumption that all human beings are in principle capable of rational thought, and that all political problems are therefore, in principle, capable of rational solution. This means that liberal solutions to questions of justice cannot appeal to non-rational or arbitrary criteria. There are three options open to the liberal theorist in the face of this double challenge. The first is to conclude that the only liberal solution is to have complete freedom of international movement – open, rather than coercive, borders.[5] The second is to argue that there are criteria for settling the membership question in a way that respects both the principles of equality and rationality, and these will be based on some value or set of values central to the liberal tradition such as equality itself, freedom, welfare or some notion of the 'nation' which can be morally and rationally grounded.[6] The third option is to accept that there are no non-arbitrary criteria for settling the membership question, but argue that it must nevertheless be settled. The need for political community overrides the need for rational criteria for membership, and so the membership question must be settled by appeal to non-rational criteria.

My objection to coercive borders has been based on a defence of the equality principle, but what I have overlooked is the third option, a move against the rationality principle. This takes the form of arguing that some level of contingency is inevitable in political theory. This contingency enters at different levels and different places in different approaches, but the point is that there are some dimensions of political life that cannot be theorized, and it is those dimensions that are at the core of justifications of coercive borders. If that move is successful, it may be that my critique of the liberal defence of coercive borders fails, because that critique assumes the relevance of the rationality principle. And so the focus of this paper is on the argument that some level of arbitrariness or contingency is inevitable in political theory when it comes to nations, membership and migration, and that it is acceptable to use some arbitrary or contingent feature as the foundation, or starting point, for a moral justification for coercive borders.

I want to distinguish this argument from what I have described above as the anti-theoretical, irrational rejection of argument and evidence by many in the public sphere who oppose immigration. It is importantly different in two ways. First, these theorists are not anti-immigration, but rather believe that individual states have the right to control immigration – many of them think that immigration regimes should be far more open than they are in practice. Second, this specific approach is not anti-theoretical, but seeks to identify the untheorizable. There are aspects of human existence that lie beyond the scope of theory – certain beliefs and practices are not irrational, but are rather non-rational. We can give no reason for them, but they are indispensable aspects of our identity and our existence. This kind of boundary is not so much imposed as discovered. The question here is whether any such boundary exists in political theory when it comes to membership and migration. There is, therefore, a considerable distance between the theoretically non-rational, the view that beliefs, principles and practices have to be taken as given to provide the starting points and foundations for theory, and the irrational anti-theoretical, the rejection of argument and evidence simply because they contradict one's beliefs about the world.

Three points of clarification are required before I begin. First, this is not an issue of arbitrary or contingent factors entering into arguments without being detected – rather, the arguments openly and explicitly aim to give a fundamental role to arbitrary or contingent factors. Second, I will not go through myriad examples of theorists who participate in the debate about the ethics of immigration and point out when and where they use this tactic – that would be a turgid exercise. Instead, I am going to focus mostly on three writers who have made important contributions of this kind to the debate: Michael Blake, Samuel Scheffler and David Miller.[7] Third, in the discussion that follows, I refer to factors and arrangements that are arbitrary or contingent from the point of view of the principles of equality and rationality. One question is whether there is a significant difference here between arbitrariness and contingency in this discussion. The 'arbitrary' is normally understood to be that which arises through random processes, a matter of pure luck, while the contingent, by contrast, can be intended and planned but could have been intended and planned differently. But whether certain arrangements are arbitrary in the strong sense or merely weakly contingent is as clear as mud, and the two terms tend to get used interchangeably. The reality is that borders do not fall where they are through purely random processes but through intention and planning; and which side of a border one is born on requires some intention and planning on the part of one's parents. I'm not sure that much hangs on making the distinction between the arbitrary and the contingent here. What does seem plausible is that certain political arrangements are morally and rationally contingent, some in such a strong sense that we are justified in describing them as arbitrary. What that amounts to saying is that as a matter of fact, they could be different from the way they are, and as a matter of rationality and ethics, there is no good reason why they have to be this way. The question for the purposes of this paper is whether arrangements like this can be used to provide a moral and rational justification for coercive borders.

One starting point for our exploration is the national border. It could be argued that we have to take the practice of national borders as given in order to do political theory at all – to imagine otherwise is to move to such a radically different political world that we require a completely new way of doing political theory that would have no grasp on a critique of political arrangements as we find them, and so would make political theory irrelevant. But as a matter of political practice, where national borders lie is a historical contingency – they have not been fixed by a practice that could be described as ethical or rational from a liberal point of view.[8] This seems relevant for the debate about the ethics of migration, because it is not merely on which side of the border one finds oneself that is arbitrary from a moral point of view, but also where that border falls and how it got there.

The point of raising the arbitrariness of borders is, of course, that national borders and national membership are connected. It is one's relationship with the territorial space contained within the border that plays some role in determining membership. This raises a worrying concern because now the ethical and rational arbitrariness of territorial borders is connected with national membership. This challenge can get radical, because if this follows for the morality of membership, it follows for other questions of justice too – why should the key obligations of justice stop at the national border? The answer has to be because we only owe those obligations to co-members, but if we can't settle on a rational and ethical way to distinguish between members and outsiders, then the whole project of liberal justice rests on a fundamental incoherence.

This is perhaps why John Rawls, in *The Law of Peoples*, is so adamant on the irrelevance of the question. There he says that boundaries are 'historically arbitrary' but their role can be justified – 'to fix on their arbitrariness is to fix on the wrong thing'. He concludes: 'There *must* be boundaries of some kind, which when viewed in isolation will seem arbitrary, and depend to some degree on historical circumstances' (Rawls 2001, p. 39). So we have to start somewhere, and that somewhere has to be boundaries of membership. The problem with this answer is that if we start here, then we start with national boundaries that have been fixed not only in arbitrary ways, but also in deeply immoral ones, so how can a theory of justice rest on *these* borders?[9] Also notice Rawls says that there must be boundaries of *some* kind, and I have no disagreement with that claim: the question is not whether there must be boundaries of some kind, but whether there should be boundaries of *this* kind. There are all sorts of boundaries that mark out the political world, which set out distinct territories that contain authorities such as nations, regions and councils, and these authorities have responsibility for democratic processes, taxation and public services but do not have coercive boundaries – people can cross freely in order to work and reside. Coercive boundaries such as national borders are comparatively rare.

Michael Blake defends Rawls' position here, arguing that for Rawls, '... membership is not itself a good whose distribution is to be evaluated by distributive justice; membership in a territorial state is required before his theory of distributive justice has applicability' (Blake 2012). And *The Law of Peoples* '... allows for inequalities between states, even if the borders between them are arbitrary and the distribution of people between them is morally arbitrary; this reflects not a refusal to apply liberalism to international justice, but a particular vision of how the notion of justice ought to be understood' (Blake 2012). Certainly, Rawls must remove the question of membership from the question of distributive justice in order for his theory to get started, but many might think this means that it starts in the wrong place, and that it doesn't so much constitute a refusal to apply liberal theory to questions of international justice, but a fundamental failure to grasp the very question of international justice.

Blake himself makes an interesting contribution that brings arbitrariness into the centre of the debate. He argues that arbitrary factors can give rise to differences that are morally relevant (Blake 2005, p. 227). He concedes that my membership of a nation is arbitrary from the moral point of view, in that it is 'produced by circumstances for which I can take neither credit nor blame'. However, '... from the fact that the circumstances giving rise to a social or political difference are arbitrary, we cannot conclude that that difference is morally *irrelevant*' (Blake 2005, p. 227). The fact is that no matter how arbitrarily constructed, the national border 'marks out something of great moral significance. It marks out, among other things, the boundaries of shared liability to a political state' (Blake 2005, p. 227). I not only have rights and entitlements against the state, but it also has rights and entitlements against me.

> If I am subject to the coercive political actions of a state, and you merely *seek* to become subject, it does not seem that you and I will necessarily be entitled to the same sort of justification from the state in question. The contingency in the world creates a difference with some moral relevance ... (Blake 2005, p. 228)

What follows from this is that: 'While one's status as a citizen might ultimately be causally determined by arbitrary facts in the world, the status of citizen does create some distinct demands for justification' (Blake 2005, p. 228). A political system, in order to be legitimate, owes certain guarantees to those who fall under its authority. Those guarantees do not apply to those who are not subject to that authority. And so arbitrary differences in circumstances create a difference in political rights. 'This difference, moreover, does not offend moral equality in the slightest' (Blake 2005, p. 229).

Differences in the right to mobility also, therefore, do not offend moral equality, if they rest on this difference of shared liability to the state. To deny the right of a citizen of the USA to move from Buffalo to Boston, for example, would be fundamentally illiberal, given the political relationship in question. But it is not fundamentally illiberal to prevent a Canadian citizen from emigrating from Toronto to live in Boston. This will have negative consequences for the would-be migrant, but is not an affront to his moral equality.

> Given that he does not live under the authority of the United States, but asks admittance to that status, it seems a mistake to consider him as equivalent to those who *already* stand in such a relationship of political authority. (Blake 2005, p. 229)

However, Blake's argument here only works if he makes the same move he attributes to Rawls, and that is to remove the question of *membership* from the issue of distributive justice. I have argued that the ethical challenge to immigration controls not only is based on concerns of distributive justice across borders but also goes much deeper (see Cole 2012). The question of distribution is not primarily to do with welfare, property or other resources, but with the membership that carries rights to those resources. It is the ethical coherence of the distinction between citizens and outsiders which is at stake, not merely that citizens of a particular state may enjoy undeservedly better life prospects than an outsider. In Blake's approach, membership of a state is the theoretical starting point, but this is a particular kind of membership and of a particular kind of state – citizenship of a liberal democratic nation-state. What we can see, then, is that the starting point of the argument, the 'given', is not made up of some core, fundamental basic concepts or ideas, but is packed with complex assumptions about the nature of the political/legal order of things, some of which seem to be highly localized to particular places and particular times.

I will return to this theme of what is included in the 'given' towards the end of the paper. For now, we should note that in many coercive-border arguments, the members/non-members boundary is given as the starting point of the argument rather than being given a moral justification. This, I have always assumed, is ruled out by the rationality principle. But Rawls and Blake argue that this is a permissible move: the members/non-members boundary *is* just given, and serves as the starting point of the argument for coercive borders without the need for a deeper moral justification – the rationality principle has no purchase here. However, earlier in his essay, Blake argues that the question of immigration raises particular difficulties for liberal political theory:

> We cannot here ask: what would we agree to, around here, as principles of political justice which respect our moral equality? And we cannot ask this because the present question is: who shall be admitted to this political we in the first place? (Blake 2005, p. 229)

For Blake, this question of admittance to the political 'we' raises issues for the methodology of liberal political theory, but if I am right, it raises irresolvable problems all the way through liberal theory's approach to migration and membership.[10]

My second example of a theorist who sees the arbitrary or contingent as playing a fundamental role in the debate is Samuel Scheffler (Scheffler 2007). On the face of it, Scheffler provides a robust critique of the role of culture in the immigration debate, rejecting the view that immigration can pose difficult challenges to a 'distinctive national culture and identity' (Scheffler 2007, p. 94). The basic problem is that cultural identification is too complicated to pose an opposition between a 'host' culture and an 'immigrant' one. Our connections with others are too complex to be reduced to a determinate cultural identity: 'the idea that each person's most fundamental identification or identifications must have their source in some fixed and determinate culture is simply untrue' (Scheffler 2007, p. 106). Scheffler's ideal is 'Hercalitean pluralism', the view that cultures are always in flux and that individuals have multiple identifications and affiliations with diverse cultures (Scheffler 2007, p. 106). When it comes to immigration, this means that immigrants cannot demand that their culture be protected by their new home state. All they can demand are the requirements of justice, and this excludes cultural entitlements. And all the host country can demand of immigrants is that they uphold the duties and obligations of citizens (Scheffler 2007, pp. 110–111).

However, Scheffler backs away from full-blown Heraclitean pluralism. This is because he thinks that people have 'strong conservative impulses', so that they seek to preserve whatever it is they value, and this includes 'present practices, forms of social organization, and ways of life' (Scheffler 2007, p. 106). So there has to be some kind of accommodation between Heraclitean pluralism and this conservative impulse (Scheffler 2007, p. 107). This compromise of pure Heraclitean pluralism is at its strongest when it comes to a *national* culture. There must be a 'political and civic culture' which is shared by everyone, and which the state must coerce citizens into preserving, and this political and civic culture is connected to the 'broader national culture', such that 'in demanding obedience to its laws and support for its institutions the state is, in effect, requiring citizens to contribute to the preservation of that culture' (Scheffler 2007, p. 112). The public political culture 'cannot be treated by the state as just one culture among others, nor can the state be expected to refrain from deploying its coercive power in support of a national culture' (Scheffler 2007, p. 113). Nor can we reasonably insist that the public political culture be devoid of any particular ethnic or linguistic elements (Scheffler 2007, p. 113). Instead, the state will have no alternative but to enforce practices and values that '… have their origins in the contingent history and traditions of a particular set of people' (Scheffler 2007, p. 113). This concern with culture takes us to the need for some policy of integration that the state has the right to enforce upon immigrants.

Scheffler recognizes the danger that policies aimed to enforce a particular culture, even a national one, could be 'based on false or incoherent ideas about the possibility of inhibiting cultural change', and claims that this problem 'lies not in the conservative impulse itself, but rather in the assessment of how best to act on it' (Scheffler 2007, p. 106). But this is a problem of process – the 'contingent history and traditions of a particular set of people' are seen as unproblematic in their content. Scheffler allows, indeed insists, that a national culture is morally and rationally contingent, but does not see that a national culture could be, not merely non-rational, but irrational. It might be replied that the problem of 'irrational' national cultures is not one that infects liberal democracies, but such a view would be extremely naïve. This problem of irrationality is endemic in national histories and traditions, including those of liberal states.[11] And so we have to ask to what extent an 'irrational' national history and the customs and traditions based upon it can be used as the basis for any coherent philosophical positions regarding the relationship between 'natives' and 'migrants'?

David Miller is one writer who faces up to something like this challenge.[12] Miller's central assertion in *On Nationality* is that a national identity can be both rationally and ethically defensible: 'it may properly be part of someone's identity that they belong to this or that national grouping' (Miller 1995, p. 10). Miller does recognize that myth makes up a significant part of national identities, and that they do not stand up to rational judgement. However, we should not think that, because of this non-rational element, they cannot play any role in ethical and political thought: '… it may not be rational to discard beliefs, even if they are, strictly speaking, false, when they can be shown to contribute significantly to the support of valuable social relations' (Miller 1995, p. 36). The fact is that national myths play a valuable role, providing reassurance that we are members of a national community that has its roots in history, connecting us up with previous generations. As such, 'they perform a moralizing role, by holding before us the virtues of our ancestors and encouraging us to live up to them' (Miller 1995, p. 36).

Miller, then, thinks the rational and ethical justification of refusing to discard beliefs one knows to be false is that they help support valuable social relations. We continue to hold a belief we know to be false because that belief makes the national identity valuable for us – it leads us to value our nation and ourselves, and helps us to feel good about the national project. But notice that if we know that these beliefs are false, we must know what actually happened to make them so – we must know the true history of the nation. And so in continuing to act as though these beliefs were true, we at the same time act as though the true set of events never happened. We can assume that these events must be unpalatable in order for us to go to the extent of fabricating an alternative narrative that we know to be false. Such fabrication could only be rationally and morally defensible if the national project is so valuable that any unpalatable facts must be 'forgotten' and new fictions created to replace them and this fabrication is necessary to save it.

Miller moves on from considering false beliefs, and claims instead that national myths more often fill in empty spaces: 'Normally the imagined history fills in blanks where no direct evidence is (or even could be) available' (Miller 1995, p. 37). Now it is not so much that there are unpalatable events in the national history that we need to 'forget' or re-tell in more digestible form – rather, there is simply the need to fill an empty space in the narrative of the nation. For Miller, what matters is not whether national stories are true or false, but whether 'national identities emerge through open processes of debate and discussion to which everyone is a potential contributor, and identities that are authoritatively imposed by repression and indoctrination' (Miller 1995, p. 39). If they are the former, 'while some elements may be mythical they are very unlikely indeed to invoke the outright denial of historical fact' (Miller 1995, p. 39). In the end, for Miller, 'the historical accuracy of national stories seems to matter less in its own right than for the effect it has in the nation's present self-understanding' (Miller 1995, p. 39).

Rather than historical accuracy, what matters for Miller is that the national story is *authentic*, in the sense of being open to input from all sections of the community. Miller's rationality and morality test for national histories has little to do with content and everything to do with process – it is one that arises from a free and equal contestation, with little or no manipulation by powerful elites. But we have to remember that in constituting the 'we' of a national story, we at the same time constitute a 'they', and this happens without democratic consultation with those constituted as 'other'. It is important for Miller then that the common public culture is a site of free and equal contestation between groups, but there is a radical sense in which this cannot happen, in that those constituted as 'outsiders' by the group have either had their input into the process ignored or have had no input at all. What we have here is a picture of the process of constituting a national identity as one dimensional, simply a matter of inclusion. But this is simply not true. What is vital to the process of national identity is the ability to distinguish one's nationality from others. As J. A. Armstrong says: '... groups tend to define themselves not by reference to their own characteristics but by exclusion, that is, by comparison to "strangers"' (Armstrong 1982, p. 5). The process of creating a national identity therefore has two elements. The first is the construction of a set of values that all members of the nation are taken to share such that they have a crucial *sameness*, setting aside the fact they do not all share these values. The second is the claim that national 'others' cannot share those values because they are *different*, again setting aside the fact that these values are widespread beyond the national border. Just as members of the nation create a fictional account of themselves, they create a fictional account of others – it is, importantly, a process of *exclusion*. And we can also see that the members do not only create a fictional account of the past, they also create a fictional account of the present. The fabrication is of the presence or absence of others in the national history and the national here-and-now.

All these sit very uneasily with the ideal of the liberal democratic political community. How can it be *ethical* to replace awkward truths with easy falsehoods? How can it be *rational* to replace the version of history we know to be true with one we know to be false, and act as if the false one was the truth? What is so valuable about the national history that we could ever be morally and rationally justified in doing this? It may be acceptable when the very life of the nation is at risk, and Miller does use the example of the Dunkirk 'myth' in British history, the evacuation of British troops from mainland Europe in 1940 (Miller 1995, p. 36). But such an example cannot ground the general liberal democratic practice of 'myth'-making Miller is describing here. Not only was the life of the nation in grave danger, normal democratic practices were suspended, and the myth of the great victory of the Dunkirk evacuation was not one the British people chose to believe, but one they were fed by the political authorities at the time.[13] Such an example of political propaganda cannot ground the general liberal democratic practice of myth-making Miller is describing here.

Conclusion

In this paper, I have drawn attention to the role of the arbitrary in the philosophical debate about immigration, the role of unreason. I have distinguished this from the role of irrationality in the public sphere, the refusal by some participants in the political debate about immigration to address arguments and evidence that contradict their view. I am not suggesting that the theorists who appeal to the legitimacy of 'unreason' in the philosophical debate are guilty of any equivalent form of irrationality. Indeed I am taking their claims very seriously, and especially the central claim, that the rationality principle has a limited role to play here. The argument is that there are some elements of the theoretical debate that we have to take as given: there are aspects of human existence that lie beyond the scope of theory. Certain beliefs and practices are not irrational, but are rather non-rational; we can give no reason for them, but they are indispensable aspects of our identity and our existence, and so constitute the starting point for theory, or essential building blocks in the overall structure.

However, when it comes to the debate about the ethics of immigration controls, we are hardly dealing with deep-seated, core beliefs and principles that we can't do without. We are dealing with national borders, nation-states, political membership – political arrangements that are not just morally and rationally contingent, but also historically contingent. We are dealing with idealized models of political institutions that have had a relatively short lifespan and which are evolving and changing all the time. We have to decide whether *these* kinds of morally and rationally contingent arrangements can play a role in the justification of coercive borders – that justification being that coercive borders are necessary in order to preserve these kinds of political arrangements. However, none of the theorists we have looked at argue that we cannot subject national borders, nation-states, membership practices or national histories as we find them to some degree of moral and rational critique. All of them are critical of actual practices of immigration and membership controls. Their claim, rather, is that there have to be boundaries of *some* kind, political institutions of *some* kind, membership rules of *some* kind, national identities of *some* kind. The moral and rational critique has to stop somewhere in order for theory to start.

But the starting point has to be subjected to moral and rational criticism in order to act as a legitimate starting point. These arrangements and features of the political landscape are not *just* starting points for theory, they are also *justifications* for other practices such as coercive borders – we need coercive borders to protect these arrangements and features. We therefore need to know that they are morally valuable in themselves. The fact remains that these writers *do* subject their starting points to moral and rational criticism, just of a limited scope. Perhaps, there is an appeal to the reasonable here – it would be unreasonable to go too far in our critique, to demand that the *very ideas* of the nation-state, the national border, national membership, national identity, be subjected to radical criticism. We cannot move beyond them to a post-national world with transnational belonging and remain within the limits of liberal political theory. As Blake points out, liberal theory has developed in the context of the nation-state. However, it does not follow from the fact that it developed within that context that it cannot or should not imagine anything beyond it. Some have argued that we need to consider forms of membership that transcend nation-states, such as membership of the international political community. This is a radical idea, and as Antoine Pécoud and Paul de Guchteneire note this kind of international mobility is a challenge for democracy: '… one needs to find ways to conciliate freedom of movement with the functioning of democratic institutions'. But they do not believe this places an insoluble obstacle in the way of establishing freedom of movement. 'A creative solution to these issues is to unpack citizenship and consider that its different components (political, civil, social, family and cultural rights notably) can be distributed in a differentiated way. This approach avoids the binary logic of exclusion, in which people have either all rights or none' (Pécoud and de Guchteneire 2005, p. 16). Ryan Pevnick also argues that the rights and duties of citizenship are not an all-or-nothing bundle – they can be, and often are, disaggregated (Pevnick 2009, p. 155).

Harold Kleindschmidt thinks that a more radical step would be to unpack the nation-state itself. He cites the work of Yasmin Soysal, who has argued for a deterritorialized 'personhood' as the basis for the allocation of citizenship rights rather than nationality (Kleinschmidt 1996, p. 13). This would be a 'postnational' model of citizenship that 'confers upon every person the right and duty of participation in the authority structures and public life of a polity, regardless of their historical or cultural ties to that community' (Soysal 1994, p. 4, Kleinschmidt 1996, p. 13), a cosmopolitan ideal of citizenship, which captures Robert Fine's principle that 'human beings can belong anywhere …' (Fine 2007, p. x). This is to look towards an idea of membership of a global political community, such that to be a free and equal member of that global community, to be an equally powerful participant within it, is deeply connected with one's freedom of mobility throughout it. This is admittedly a sketchy vision. But as Duncan Ivison observes: 'I take it that one of the great projects of twenty-first-century political thought is to develop new models of transnational and global political order that can provide not only effective security and welfare provision for citizens, but that can also become the object of people's reasoned loyalty; to construct, in other words, new forms of transnational democracy' (Ivison 2008, p. 212).[14]

Also, we must be aware that the discussion of the ethics of migration takes place in the context of a power relationship between the 'inside' (the developed world) and the 'outside' (the developing world), such that the developed world uses a global migration regime to exploit the global poor. The reality is that we are not – or should not be – discussing the rights of a particular liberal state to control movement across its borders. We are talking about a global migration regime, through which a block of powerful liberal capitalist states seek to prevent access for the poor and unskilled while exploiting their labour at cheap costs where they happen to be; and also actively seeking out those it considers economically valuable from the poor world to meet their own needs, creating more difficulties for 'sending' states in terms of the 'brain drain'; and maintaining more or less free movement between themselves as a block. This migration regime plays a role not only in maintaining extreme inequalities of wealth across the globe, but also extreme inequalities of global power.

The danger of taking particular contingent or arbitrary arrangements as legitimate starting points or essential building blocks for political philosophy when it comes to questions of migration and membership is that those starting points are imbued with these power relations, and by histories of colonial oppression and exploitation. The body of theory produced represents the perspective of the citizen who is theorizing the migrant as a problem that needs solving. What may be overlooked is the perspective of the migrant, for whom the citizen is a problem that needs solving. Theory is being produced, not in a neutral space, but from a privileged position in a power structure. A body of theory constructed in the space of migrancy might look radically different from that constructed within the privileged space of the academia of the developed North.

Liberal political theory has privileged the voice of the insider. It may be that those who devise these 'insider'-theories have a theoretical justification for doing so, but my suspicion is that any such justification begs the fundamental question, the moral validity of the boundary between the inside and the outside. The way in which the privileging of the voice of the insider is deeply ingrained within political theory is shown by Seyla Benhabib's use of discourse ethics to establish a human right to membership. Her discourse between the insider and the outsider goes as follows (note that from the beginning she, as the speaker, is the insider):

> If you and I enter into a moral dialogue with one another, and if I am a member of a state of which you are seeking membership and you are not, then I must be able to show you with good grounds, grounds that would be acceptable to each of us equally, why you can never join our association and become one of us. These must be grounds that you would accept if you were in my situation and I were in yours. Our reasons must be reciprocally acceptable; they must apply to us equally. (Benhabib 2004, p. 138)

In order to be acceptable, such grounds would be to do with qualifications, skills and resources (Benhabib 2004, p. 139). But note that the crucial aspect of the discourse is that *these must be grounds that you would accept if you were in my situation*. In other words, the outsider must think from the perspective of the insider, and so once more the perspective of the insider is privileged. The sentence should at least read: *These must be grounds that you would accept if you were in my situation and I would accept if I were in yours*. As it stands, there is no reciprocity here. If the grounds for exclusion are to be genuinely 'acceptable to us equally', then they have to be acceptable to the outsider *as outsider*. And equally importantly, they must be contested against grounds for *inclusion* which must carry equal weight in the exchange.

Lori Watson points out:

> The emphasis on reasons we could not reasonably reject as the standard of moral justification requires us to recognize that such reasons have the character they do, in part, because they are reasons we can share – as moral equals. Acknowledging that immigrants stand in a political relationship vis-à-vis the state of intended migration requires acknowledging that the state is obligated to offer justifications that could not be reasonably rejected for its principles. This, however, also requires acknowledging the immigrant as a reason-giver in this context, and as an equal. (Watson 2008, p. 988)

But for the migrant to be an equal in this exchange, in order for us to give reasons from positions of equality, we have to be prepared to think outside of the conventional political frameworks that position the migrant as the 'problem' figure in this relationship.

I have always argued that the question of membership poses a radical challenge for liberal political theory as such – it is not a marginal issue, such that it can be dealt with, so that we can carry on with business as usual. Instead, liberal theory cannot address the membership question without addressing itself, and cannot answer it without radically transforming itself (Cole 2000, p. 202). Michael Blake recognizes this when he says:

> We cannot here ask: what would we agree to, around here, as principles of political justice which respect our moral equality? And we cannot ask this because the present question is: who shall be admitted to this political we in the first place? (Blake 2005, p. 226)

And he importantly recognizes that this means that:

> An adequate analysis of immigration … requires a fundamental revision of the methodology of liberal political philosophy. Immigration is not simply one more issue to which the machinery of liberal political philosophy might be applied; by its very nature, it forces the revision of some of the assumptions traditionally made by liberal theorists. (Blake 2005, p. 224)

But I think that the revision of liberal political philosophy is far more funda-mental than he allows. In the end, what we are being asked to accept by the approaches I have considered in this paper is that the intrinsic worth of contin-gent and arbitrary features of the political world such as national borders, nation-states and national identities outweigh the non-contingent moral equality of the migrant (see Tonkiss 2013, p. 53). However, if the migrant is to be rec-ognized as an equal reason-giver in the moral contestation of borders, then the conception of the just global order and the place of the nation-state within it have to be radically revised. Rather than being a marginal figure in liberal political theory, the migrant compels us to question its very foundations and imagine a new vision of a global political community, a post-national world made up of transnational belonging.

Acknowledgement

I would like to thank Patti T. Lenard and Crispino Akakpo for the helpful feedback and encouraging comments on earlier drafts of this paper, and for the constructive comments from the anonymous referee. I presented versions of this paper to the Institute for Research into Superdiversity (IRiS) at the University of Birmingham, and the Social Ethics Research Group at the University of South Wales. Thanks to Nando Sigona, Katherine Tonkiss, Luis Cabrera, Gideon Calder and Steve Smith in particular for valu-able feedback at those events.

Notes

1. For evidence that European Union migrants to the United Kingdom between 2004 and 2008 made a positive contribution to public finances, despite the UK running a budget deficit, see http://migrationobservatory.ox.ac.uk/briefings/fiscal-impact-immigration-uk [Accessed 4 April 2014]. Also see Joakim Ruist, 'the fisal conse-quences of unrestricted immigration from Romania and Bulgaria', 18 January 2014, http://www.voxeu.org/article/immigration-romania-and-bulgaria-fiscal-impact [Accessed 4 April 2014]. On the relationship between immigration and crime, see Ceobanu (2011) and Lynch and Simon (1999). For more recent data, see http://www.migrationobservatory.ox.ac.uk/briefings/immigration-and-crime-evidence-uk-and-other-countries [Accessed 4 April 2014].
2. In identifying the role of irrationality here, I am not suggesting that it must be irra-tional to attribute values to being a member of a community, and to seek to con-trol membership of that community in order to preserve those values. I am simply pointing to the extent to which some elements of the public sphere who are hostile to immigration refuse to engage with any argument and evidence that contradicts their view. Thanks to Patti L. Lennard for asking me to clarify this.
3. See Cole (2014) where I do discuss the 'mythology' of borders in the public debate, and the possible sources of the mythology in the idea of 'Heimat'. For the state of anti-immigration politics, see Higham (2006) and Betz (1993).
4. See in particular Cole (2012), Cole (2011) and Cole (2000).
5. I think the contrast between open and coercive borders is more accurate than a contrast between open and closed borders. Very few of the theorists who argue against the open borders position can be understood as advocating anything like a

closed-borders position, but they are all, to some degree, arguing for coercive borders.

6. One of the most recent interesting approaches has been to base the argument on the right of freedom of association – see Wellman (2011). For a critique of this approach, see Cole (2011) pp. 233–260, and Fine (2010).

7. I am also not suggesting that this is the *only* move they make in the debate – it is *one* move among many that they propose as counter-arguments to open borders.

8. An extreme example is the way in which nation-state borders were fixed in Africa by the colonial powers at the Berlin conference in 1884–1885. In 1890, Lord Salisbury, the British Prime Minister, commented on the process: 'we have been engaged in drawing lines upon maps where no white man's foot ever trod; we have been giving away mountains and rivers and lakes to each other, only hindered by the small impediment that we never knew exactly where the mountains and rivers and lakes were' (Thomson 2010, p. 14).

9. Of course, the answer is that we start, not with *precisely* these, but ones without the immoral elements. I will address this reply later in the essay.

10. In a more recent work, Blake develops a 'jurisdictional' justification for the right to exclude (Blake 2013). The state has jurisdiction over a particular territorial and legal community, such that anybody who enters that jurisdiction places those already there under an obligation to extend legal protection to them. This obligation is imposed without their consent. Therefore, current inhabitants have a (limited) right to exclude unwanted migrants. Although this argument rests on similar starting assumptions about the nature of membership, I do not claim that what I have said here constitutes a reply to it, and I hope to address this highly challenging and important contribution to the debate in more detail elsewhere.

11. See Hobsbawm and Ranger (2012), and Littler and Naidoo (2005).

12. But he emphasizes *public* culture as the condition of citizenship, and so wouldn't go so far as Scheffler here, although he does argue that citizen-testing on that public culture is morally permissible – see Miller (2008).

13. See Major General J. F. C. Fuller's account written in 1948 (Fuller 1993). And see Harmon's *Dunkirk: The Patriotic Myth* (1980). See also Calder's *The Myth of the Blitz* (1991). James Chisum comments that, for Calder, representations of the Second World War in English national identity are 'centred on the mythological triad of Dunkirk, the Battle of Britain and the Blitz …', and 'predicated upon the acceptance and internalisation of wartime propaganda' (Chisum 2011).

14. Katherine Tonkiss has made a major contribution to theorizing migration in a post-national context. See Tonkiss (2013).

References

Armstrong, J.A., 1982. *Nations before nationalism*. Chapel Hill: University of North Carolina Press.

Benhabib, S., 2004. *The rights of others*. Cambridge: Cambridge University Press.

Betz, H., 1993. The new politics of resentment: radical right-wing populist parties in western europe. *Comparative politics*, 25 (4), 413–427.

Blake, M., 2005. Immigration. *In*: R.G. Frey and C.H. Wellman, eds. *A companion to applied ethics*. Oxford: Blackwell, 224–237.

Blake, M., 2012. Review of C. H. Wellman and P. Cole, 2011. *Debating the ethics of immigration: is there a right to exclude?* New York: Oxford University Press. Notre Dame Philosophical Reviews. Available from: http://ndpr.nd.edu/news/32280-debating-the-ethics-of-immigration-is-there-a-right-to-exclude/ [Accessed 27 June 2013].

Blake, M., 2013. Immigration, jurisdiction, and exclusion. *Philosophy and public affairs*, 41, 103–130.

Calder, A., 1991. *The myth of the blitz*. London: Pimlico.

Ceobanu, A.M., 2011. Usual suspects? Public views about immigrants' impact on crime in European countries. *International journal of comparative sociology*, 52, 114–131.

Chisum, J., 2011. Angus calder's the myth of the blitz. *E-international relations*. Available from: http://www.e-ir.info/2011/06/01/angus-calders-'the-myth-of-the-blitz/ [Accessed 4 April 2014].

Cole, P., 2000. *Philosophies of exclusion: liberal political theory and immigration*. Edinburgh: Edinburgh University Press.

Cole, P., 2011. Open borders: an ethical defense. *In*: C.H. Wellman and P. Cole, eds. *Debating the ethics of immigration: is there a right to exclude?* New York: Oxford University Press, 159–313.

Cole, P., 2012. Taking moral equality seriously: egalitarianism and immigration controls. *Journal of international political theory*, 8, 121–134.

Cole, P., 2014. Reason, myth and migration. *INLOGOV blog: official blog of the institute of local government studies*. University of Birmingham. Available from: http://inlogov.wordpress.com/2014/01/20/reason-myth-migration/?utm_source=twitterfeed&utm_medium=twitter [Accessed April 4, 2014].

Fine, R., 2007. *Cosmopolitanism*. London: Routledge.

Fine, S., 2010. Freedom of association is not the answer. *Ethics*, 120, 338–356.

Fuller, J.F.C., 1993. *The second world war: a strategical and tactical history*. Cambridge: Da Capo Press.

Goodhart, D., 2013. *The british dream: successes and failures of postwar immigration*. London: Atlantic Books.

Harmon, N., 1980. *Dunkirk: the patriotic myth*. New York: Simon and Schuster.

Higham, J., 2006. Patterns in the making. *In*: A.M. Messina and G. Lahav, eds. *The migration reader: exploring politics and policies*. Boulder: Lynne Rienner, 375–383.

Hobsbawm, E. and Ranger, T., eds., 2012. *The invention of tradition*. Cambridge: Cambridge University Press.

Ivison, D., 2008. *Rights*. Stocksfield: Acumen.

Kleinschmidt, H., 1996. *Migration and the making of transnational social spaces*. Public address to Australian Centre, University of Melbourne. Available from: http://spatialaesthetics.unimelb.edu.au/static/files/assets/55c7d377/Kleinschmidt_-_Migration_and_the_Making_of_Transnational_Social_Spaces.pdf [Accessed 24 August 2010].

Littler, J. and Naidoo, R., eds., 2005. *The politics of heritage: the legacies of 'race'*. London: Routledge.

Lynch, J.P. and Simon, R.J., 1999. A comparative assessment of criminal involvement among immigrants and natives across seven nations. *International criminal justice review*, 9, 1–17.

Miller, D., 1995. *On nationality*. Oxford: Clarendon Press.

Miller, D., 2008. Immigrants, nations, and citizenship. *Journal of political philosophy*, 16, 371–390.

Pécoud, A. and de Guchteneire, P., 2005. Migration without borders: an investigation into the free movement of people. *Global migration perspectives no 27*, Global Commission on International Migration, Geneva, Switzerland.

Pevnick, R., 2009. Social trust and the ethics of immigration policy. *Journal of political philosophy*, 17, 146–167.

Portes, J., 2013. An exercise in scapegoating. *The London review of books*, 35, 7–9.

Rawls, J., 2001. *The law of peoples*. Cambridge: Harvard University Press.

Scheffler, S., 2007. Immigration and the significance of culture. *Philosophy & public affairs*, 35, 93–125.

Soysal, Y., 1994. *Limits of citizenship: migrants and postnational membership in Europe*. Chicago, IL: Chicago University Press.

Thomson, A., 2010. *An introduction to African politics*. 3rd ed. London: Routledge.

Tonkiss, K., 2013. *Migration and identity in a post-national world*. Basingstoke: Palgrave Macmillan.

Watson, L., 2008. Equal justice: comment on michael blake's immigration and political equality. *San Diego law review*, 45, 981–988.

Wellman, C.H., 2011. Freedom of association and the right to exclude. *In*: C.H. Wellman and P. Cole, eds. *Debating the ethics of immigration: is there a right to exclude?* New York: Oxford University Press, 13–155.

The right to exclude

Michael Blake

Department of Philosophy and Daniel J. Evans School of Public Affairs, University of Washington, Seattle, WA, USA

Many contemporary theories of immigration begin with the idea that we obtain the right to exclude, because there are some goods that can be produced only within bounded societies. I believe these views to be mistaken, both ethically and empirically. More plausible accounts of the right to exclude begin with the idea that individuals have rights, in virtue of their moral rights of association or of property, to avoid admitting foreigners into their societies. I believe these accounts have to be amended to make reference to the juridical nature of the modern state. My own view is that the right to exclude is grounded in the right to avoid becoming the agent charged with the defense of another's human rights – unless there is some independent moral reason one ought to become so charged. This account is able to ground the right to exclude, but does not justify the ways in which modern states employ that putative right.

The question of exclusion is the first question to be asked about the morality of immigration. It is emphatically not the *only* question that must be asked. It has the same relationship to questions of immigration as the justification of punishment does to a host of more specific questions about criminal law; it sets the scope of acceptable solutions, as it were, by specifying what sorts of practices and policies have a hope of being justifiable. (And, in both cases, if one is an abolitionist, it sets the stage for the rejection of *all* such practices and policies.) No one, though, should expect that all interesting questions of criminal justice could be solved with reference to a theory of punishment; even if we accept a retributive account of punishment, that is, we might still need to think very hard about whether current practices of criminal punishment are morally rightful. So it is, I think, for immigration. Those of us who are not abolitionists about immigration controls – who think that liberal states have the right to engage in at least some practices of exclusion – are still likely to have further questions about the permissibility of current immigration law. There are many questions to be asked, and a theory of exclusion can provide at best limited answers.

I am therefore heartened to see the variety of topics discussed in this volume. My own focus, however, will be a narrow one. I want to do two things in the present essay. I want, first, to examine some contemporary discussions of the right to exclude. I will not pretend to be neutral; I defend a particular vision of the right to exclude, which I refer to as the *jurisdictional* theory of that right. I will, however, try to be as fair as I can to competing theories, even as I give what I take to be their flaws. It is my belief that these theories share, at root, a common failing; they are insufficiently attentive to the fact that immigration involves a political change – a change, that is, in the political community charged with the defense of the human rights of the migrating person. My own view, which I will briefly lay out at the end of this essay, is an attempt to avoid this problem. My second purpose – which I will deal with only at the very end of this essay – is to examine a few issues that this theory of exclusion will find it hard, by itself, to adjudicate. I do not, of course, take this to be a flaw unique to the jurisdictional theory I defend; I think all theories of exclusion will have a similar need to be supplemented before they can answer the questions I examine.

I will begin this essay, though, by considering a few arguments to the effect that we do not need to supplement the theory of exclusion; we need, instead, to abandon it entirely.

1. Open borders

The idea that liberal states do not have the right to exclude unwanted outsiders – that the liberal state cannot, consistent with its liberalism, coercively prevent outsiders from entering into that state's territory – is conventionally referred to as the *open borders* view (Wilcox 2009). The view is not reducible to a single argument; there are a variety of arguments that have been deployed to defend the proposition that border controls ought to be abolished (see also Carens 1987, Abizadeh 2008, Huemer 2010). I will not try to canvas all possible arguments in favor of abolition here. I will, instead, focus on three plausible arguments in favor of open borders: the argument from symmetry between domestic and international mobility; the argument from symmetry between entry and exit rights; and the argument from international distributive justice. I will discuss these in turn.

1.1. The argument from symmetry between domestic and international mobility

The argument from symmetry between domestic and international mobility may be stated rather simply: if there is a value to human lives in being able to move around within a particular territorial community, then there is similarly value in being able to move around between political communities. Most of us react poorly to internal constraints on migration. The Soviet 'closed cities' – industrial and military communities, such as Kaliningrad and Vladivostok, to which domestic 'migration' was sharply controlled – were generally regarded as instruments of totalitarianism; liberal democracies could not hope to control internal migration, while still regarding themselves as legitimate (Torpey 2007). But the same human interests and needs that render internal controls illegitimate tell just as sharply against external controls; if we have reason to believe that human lives require the freedom to move in space – to pursue jobs, ground projects, and loves – then we have reason to defend this universally, rather than locally. The prohibition on internal migration, so comfortably a part of liberal morality, turns out to have unimagined consequences; we are simply incoherent if we defend the moral centrality of internal migration, while allowing the coercive prevention of external migration (Carens 1992, Wellman and Cole 2011).

The argument given here is rhetorically powerful; it forces the liberal to note that the universalism that animates her liberalism has historically been applied within only a limited territorial boundary. This should be, at the least, a reason to reconsider the easy liberal acceptance of the supposed right to exclude. The argument is, however, subject to some difficulties. Chief among these, I think, is the fact that what the two 'migrants' do, in the two cases, is different in relevant aspects. The internal migrant, who moves within her political community, is moving *within* a particular jurisdiction. She is bound, on all stages of her journey, to obey the commands of her political and legal society. The state owes her, in this, a particular duty of justification; it must justify, to her, the rightfulness of the coercive force it exercises over her. The external migrant, in contrast, is doing something rather different. She is not present within that political and legal community; rather, in her movement through space, she is trying to *become* subject to that community. The change she proposes to make is one that involves acquiring a new relationship to others – namely, the relationship of being a fellow member of a community defined by mutual legal and political obligation. It is open to the critic, then, to say that the apparent similarity between the two cases masks a deeper dissimilarity. What it is that the two are proposing to do is sufficiently different that some justifications for mobility might apply to the former, but not to the latter. Hosein (2013) has argued that the right to mobility exists as part of the pattern of justification that is owed to current residents within a particular legal community; as such, the right to mobility simply cannot be thought to apply with equal force to those who seek to *enter* that community. Indeed, I believe we ought to understand the right to mobility as something akin to the right to vote; both are part of the package of duties that a just state owes to those residents within that state's territory – but neither can be applied, simply in virtue of their usefulness to individual purposes and desires, to the world's citizens. This differentiation, moreover, does not deny the equality of persons, any more than my lack of ability to vote in French elections violates the norm that I should be treated as a moral equal by French political institutions. I am not subject to French laws, and the French political community therefore has no need to justify itself to me through electoral politics. This, however, is not a violation of equality; it is, instead, what equality itself demands (Blake 2003). Equality demands that like cases be treated alike – and, as importantly, that what is relevantly different be treated differently.

1.2. The argument from symmetry between entrance and exit rights

The right to emigrate is given enormous importance in international human rights law; the Universal Declaration of Human Rights enshrines, in Article 13, a human right to exit any country, including one's own. This right, though, is functionally useless without a country to which one can, in fact, exit. This means that – on this argument – we are either deluded in our belief that the right to exit is important; or, if we are not so deluded, we ought to recognize that all countries have the obligation to allow outsiders to enter into their communities. The right to exit, in other words, requires the right of entrance for it to be worth our while; if we respect the former – and, on this argument, we are right to do so – we are duty-bound to respect the latter (Cole 2000, Ypi 2008).

This argument is an important one. One response to it, with Christopher Heath Wellman, is to make an analogy to the right to marry: this right does not imply the right to marry any particular person, but only to marry a person who in turn wishes to marry me. Phillip Cole disputes the analogy: we are not required to have a marriage in order to have a life worth living – but every person requires a political community, if they are to have adequate protection for their basic rights (Wellman and Cole 2011, pp. 197–203). We might, then, try a different sort of response. My own view is that the rightfulness of an action depends not just upon what that act brings about in the world, but upon the relationship between the actor and the one acted upon. In justifying an act, that is, we have reason to look not just to what the act makes happen; we have reason to examine whether or not the one who acts is the right agent to so act. The nature of the agent, in other words, may sometimes transform the nature of the act.

Think, in connection with this, of the suicide of Hermann Göering. Göering committed suicide, by cyanide pill, on the night before he was to have been hanged. The pill was apparently provided to him by Private Herbert Stivers, who was under the belief that it was needed medicine. Stivers later expressed profound regret for his role in helping Göering 'cheat the hangman' (Ehrenfreund 2007, p. 91). If all that is at issue in an action's rightness is its results, then his regret is mysterious; whether Stivers acted or not, the result was the same – a dead Göering. Stivers's regret, though, is entirely comprehensible. Göering was not the right agent to administer the death in question. The Allies did not simply desire the state of affairs in which Göering was dead; they wanted him to be executed – which is to say, they wanted a particular agent to be the cause of that death. The agent, and the relationship, mattered enormously in the morality of the act.

So too, I believe, with migration controls. Suppose I am prevented from leaving my country and entering into another country. On this symmetry argument, it matters nothing whether or not the agent causing this result is my own (current) government, or the government of the society to which I seek to emigrate. In either case, I am prevented from moving, and that is detrimental to my desires, and that is all we need to know. On my view, though, there is a rather important moral difference between my being unable to move because my government won't let me *depart,* and my being unable to move because some other government won't let me *enter.* The latter represents a government refusing to enter into a particular sort of new relationship, one that begins when the would-be migrant enters into the jurisdiction ruled by that government; perhaps that government is right to do so, perhaps not. The act, though, is different in *kind* from the act of a government refusing to allow me to leave. Even if the net result is the same in both cases – I stay where I am – we are right to feel that there is a moral difference in the two cases. Legitimate governments have no right, on my view, to insist on coercively maintaining *permanence* in their relationships with their subjects. They are not allowed, consistent with their liberalism, to prevent those subjects from leaving. To admit this much, though, does not tell us anything at all about the rightness of exclusion. We are quite right to insist that the right to exit is a basic human right, even if we defend some version of the right to exclude. The state has no right to coercively include its citizens, and this is true even if no other state has a right to admit them into new membership. The coercive act of exclusion is thus morally distinct from the coercion involved in the prevention of emigration. The nature of the agents in the two cases is simply not the same, and we are right to resist the equation made in the above argument.

1.3. Open borders and global distributive justice

The last argument I want to consider for open borders is perhaps the most powerful. It begins with a simple, although often overlooked, fact: the borders of the world are not natural facts. They were, instead, set up as a result of a centuries-long process of colonization and resource theft. The borders, moreover, now currently define a line between the rich and the poor; being born on the 'right' side of the line between Mexico and the United States, or the Dominican Republic and Haiti, will determine more than anything else how well your life is likely to go. The borders, that is, function here and now to maintain an admittedly unjust pattern of resource distribution, by insisting that actual persons cannot migrate to where their expectations – for employment, for toleration, for representative democratic institutions – are superior. The practices of exclusion we use are thus the last vestige of colonial empire; if we are to live up to the universalism inherent in liberal thought, we are obligated to eliminate the practice of exclusion itself (Cole 2000).

This argument is powerful, since it harnesses the practice of exclusion to the admitted reality of global distributive injustice. It is important, though, to be precise. The argument claims two things: first, that open borders would help the world's poor; and, second, that global distributive justice would require the absence of exclusion. I believe there are significant problems with both claims. To begin with the latter: the argument depends upon the claim that exclusion *itself* is the problem – rather than some more particular pattern or practice of exclusion. But it is not clear that all forms of exclusion are in fact props for colonial privilege. Mozambique has recently seen protests over land leased to Chinese corporations, which would involve Chinese nationals working on Mozambiquan territory (Von Braun and Meizen-Dick 2009). The protest, we might note, involves the effects of the (temporary) migration of Chinese laborers onto Mozambiquan territory, and the protestors are convinced that this pattern of border crossings will decrease the already meager distributive shares for Mozambiquan workers. Whether the protestors are right or wrong is not at issue; what can be said, instead, is that these protestors' claims are plausible, and they are making claims that distributive justice is *undermined* by this particular form of migration. What we can take away from their protests is the idea that migration rights are not always a *remedy* for global underdevelopment; we cannot rest easy with the idea that global distributive justice would require the elimination of exclusion.

This leads to the first point discussed above: if we were to use whatever pattern of migration rights best conduces to global distributive justice, we would be unlikely to arrive at a program of open borders. There are at least two reasons why this is true. The first is that wealthy states do not generally become wealthy by means of natural resources; indeed, ample natural resources often lead to decidedly mixed results – the so-called 'Dutch disease' is an endemic problem for developing countries (Wenar 2008). Instead, wealth appears to be created through a mix of factors, whose precise composition is controversial, but which most certainly include the existence of political institutions that are able to avoid the traps of corruption (Easterly 2001, see also Miller 2007, p. 241). If the evidence of Collier (2008) is right, then wealth emerges where national elites are sufficiently loyal to the national community to forego maximal advantage via corruption; corruption – and the foreign willingness to incentivize corruption – tends to slow or reverse the development of low-income societies. What this means is that the opening of borders is unlikely to increase the production of wealth for low-income societies; in fact, if representative democracy requires a knowledge of who is represented and a fairly stable long-term population, then the opening of borders may in fact impede it (Song forthcoming). This is made more problematic by the second point I want to raise here: a policy of open borders is likely to have decidedly mixed results for the internal economies of developing societies. As Thomas Pogge has noted, when borders are opened, those who leave are those who are already wealthy enough to leave; the deeply impoverished are unlikely to have the resources required to emigrate (Pogge 2006). Economists who have studied the 'brain drain' have noted that the concrete effects of migration from developing societies are complex, but not universally positive (Kapur and McHale 2005). The sending of remittances from workers abroad is a powerful goad towards development (Pritchett 2006); the absent human capital, however, is likely to undermine the development of responsive political and economic institutions (Blake and Brock forthcoming). It is, finally, worth noting that the impoverished residents of developing societies might have a right to development in their societies of origin; even if greater migration rights would have beneficial effects, we should not therefore conclude that such rights should be a foundational part of our response to poverty (Oberman 2011). The policy of open borders, then, is at best one policy to be considered in response to global poverty – and it is unlikely to be the best policy considered.

2. The justification of exclusion

The above has considered arguments to the effect that exclusion is never justifiable. What I want to focus on now are those arguments to the effect that it is *sometimes* justifiable. There are, here, two distinct categories of argument: the first begins with facts of national or cultural identity, and the second upon the moral rights of individuals. The lines between the two are not sharp; many theorists invoke arguments from both categories. Nevertheless, I want to differentiate them as much as I can. I will begin with the first category; since my own view is best described as falling under the second category, I will spend more time there.

2.1. Community and exclusion

The most common ground for exclusion – both in ordinary politics and in political philosophy – goes towards the importance of the national community, and the role of immigration policy in shaping that community. There are a variety of ways in which this idea is spelled out; versions of it are found in theorists best described as communitarian, while other versions are articulated by those who understand themselves as liberal egalitarians (Walzer 1983, Kymlicka 1996). What they have in common is a belief that there are some important goods that can only be produced by something like a community – by, that is, a group of people who share certain attributes that are not shared by humanity more generally. Some theorists emphasize shared linguistic community; others emphasize more general practices of community and self-description (Kymlicka 1996, Miller 2005). These theorists emphasize that communities of character can produce important human goods, in a manner that is all too frequently ignored by the abstract individualism of liberal thought. Indeed, one very common claim is that only communities linked in such a way can produce societies able to live in accordance with the principles defended by liberalism; for liberalism to be a viable political philosophy, it must be interpreted and lived within a particular cultural and historic community (Walzer 1983, Tamir 1993, Stilz 2010). Immigration, then, is of enormous importance, since it has the potential to radically reshape the nature of the community to which emigrants journey. Where a community would be undermined by the existence of immigration – where it would not be able to produce what community produces – that community is right to exclude.

This argument has several variants, with different degrees of strength; this thumbnail, though, may allow us to proceed. The argument given here is an important one, but it has several points at which it is vulnerable to criticism. The first of these focuses on the questionable empirical premises the argument demands; the second of these looks at the theoretical structure of the argument itself.

To begin with the empirics, we might note that the argument, as stated, depends upon two things being true: namely, that some sort of commonality is needed for shared liberal community, and that exclusion is in turn needed for this sort of commonality. I am not an expert in empirical sociology, and believe philosophers should avoid pretending they possess expertise they do not (Blake 2012c). I do believe, though, that those who assume that such commonality is required for political society must come to terms with some apparent counter-examples. Look, for example, at the city of Miami. In 2000, more than two-thirds of all Miami citizens spoke Spanish as their first language; English, in contrast, was the first language of only 25% of the population (United States Census 2000). This makes Miami rather different from most cities in the United States. This difference in language, of course, brings with it a difference in media, in self-description, in cultural signifiers, and so forth; the average inhabitant of Miami is, in many ways, rather unlike the average inhabitant of Seattle. And yet two things are worth noting here: the first is that the inhabitants of Seattle and the inhabitants of Miami are, in fact, able to do politics together – or, at the very least, that they are not obviously *worse* at doing this than any other two cities joined together by a federal state. The existence of linguistic or cultural pluralism may make politics more difficult; it does not make it impossible. The second thing to note is that the border (as it were) between Seattle and Miami is as open as can be; nothing stops people from making the move across the United States. Comparatively few do, of course, and the cultural differences between the two continue to be rather stark. If this is right, though, then both empirical claims – about the necessity of what is common, and the necessity of exclusion to maintain that commonality – might be, at the very least, overstated.

This leads us to our second, more theoretical, difficulty: it is never entirely clear whether or not those who defend immigration with reference to cultural community have actually defended a *right* to exclude. At the most, given what has been said about Miami, they have identified something that is *helpful* in the pursuit of democratic identity; perhaps there are some goods that simply won't be easily produced, in a country as diverse as the United States. It is not clear, though, that this fact – if it is a fact – is enough to justify exclusion to those who are excluded. Imagine that a country will become less likely to flourish, if it is made more diverse; imagine further that I have some pressing need – perhaps I am a refugee; perhaps I am simply in love with a local – to enter into that country. For the present argument here to go through, it must be the case that the argument has established a right on the part of the state to exclude; I do not think, though, that it has. At most, it has identified something useful, something good – and those things must be made to stand up against other goods, to see which is more important. In short: even if the nationalist claims are true, they have not established a *right* to exclude.

There are more worries that can be adduced here; I have discussed some of them elsewhere (Blake 2003). Right now, though, I want to turn to a comparatively smaller set of theorists: those who have defended a right to exclude with reference to the rights of individual persons.

2.2. *Individual rights and exclusion*

In this section, I want to examine two recent arguments, each of which tries to ground the right to exclude in the rights held by individuals – to freedom of association, on the first argument, and to acquire and hold property, on the second. I believe this pattern of argument is more likely to succeed in justifying the right to exclude; much of what I say here, then, is intended to articulate a few points on which I disagree with the specifics offered by these authors. At the risk of hiding the considerable appeal of these theories, I want to use them to set up my own, jurisdictional theory in the last section of this paper.

We can start, then, with Christopher Heath Wellman's (Wellman and Cole 2011) argument from freedom of association. The argument has the virtue of comparative simplicity; it begins with the fact that individuals have the right to freely associate with others of their own choosing. To this, we add the fact that this right entails the right to be free from associating with unwanted others; my right to freedom of association is undermined if I am unable to choose those with whom I will exercise that freedom. The final piece of the puzzle is that the right applies with equal force to collectives, including states, as it does to persons. States, being made up of people, have the right to be free from forced association, whether that involves being forcibly assimilated into a larger state, or being made to take in unwanted members. In both cases, the state is free to resist the unwanted association; it is able to do this because the members of that state have the right to decide with whom they will associate, in the street and in the marketplace. Self-determination, on this view, consists in the right of a legitimate state to decide its future for itself – and that freedom includes the right to be free from unwanted association.

This is a fascinating argument, and it repays close attention. In the present context, I want to note my agreement with Wellman's idea that the right of the community to exclude is grounded in the right to be free from the imposition of an unwanted new relationship; we are right to keep this aspect of immigration at the forefront of our minds. I disagree, though, with two aspects of Wellman's argument. The first, as I have said elsewhere, is that Wellman's argument might be too strong; freedom of association is an important right, but it can be – and has been – overridden by other important purposes; as such, I do not think it is necessarily true that a strong right to exclude can be grounded in these materials (Blake 2012a). The first is the focus on the *social* relationship as the key aspect of the argument for exclusion. Wellman argues that we are permitted to exclude, when we do not want to join with the newcomer in our streets and in our marketplaces; we use the force of law to enforce this social exclusion. For my part, I would argue that what is primary is the legal relationship itself. One who crosses into my jurisdiction joins in a relationship of mutual obligation with me, whereby we are each duty bound to act in particular ways in defense of one another's rights. This, on my view, is what is worth highlighting in our theories of exclusion. The immigrant may, after all, never enter into my cultural or national community at all; indigenous Oaxacan immigrants may move across international borders while remaining within a single Oaxacan cultural community, which extends from Oaxaca proper to Los Angeles (Reed-Sandoval 2014). What is changed when such an immigrant crosses the border is not necessarily social, though it may be; it is, however, necessarily legal, given the legal importance of simple territorial presence. We ought to keep our focus on this fact, I think, and a theory that does not begin with this fact is less likely to be a successful one.

Pevnick's (2011) argument similarly begins with a notion of individual rights – specifically, here, the right to acquire property. Those people who are now members of a society have, through their labor and financial contributions, helped to create and sustain political institutions; they have, thereby, acquired a set of property rights in those institutions. They are, therefore, entitled to seek to exclude those who would enter into the territory over which such institutions hold jurisdiction. The current residents, on Pevnick's view, have acquired rights of property over the institutions governing their society; the right to exclude emerges from that set of property rights. As with Wellman, the notion of self-determination emerges from consideration of these individual rights; the self-determination of a society consists in the exercise, by its members, of rightful control over that society's institutions. That rightful control, naturally, includes the right to exclude.

As with Wellman, I am ignoring a great deal of fine detail, in a subtle and powerful argument. For the moment, I want to concentrate only on what I find difficult to accept in Pevnick's argument – namely, that the notion of property rights is an appropriate one to use in a discussion of the right of exclusion. Pevnick rests the right to exclude on something very much like a Lockean notion of property, on which those who have labored over a good obtain the right to exclude others from that good. The institutions of political justice, though, are not generally thought of as goods like any other sort of goods, to be owned, sold, or traded. On Pevnick's analysis, we might ask, what rights are enjoyed by the handicapped – those who, we might imagine, cannot labor in the marketplace, pay taxes, or otherwise establish that they have worked in support of political institutions? If Pevnick wants those individuals to have no property rights as regards the institutions of politics, and hence no particular claim to continued residency, then I think his theory is in difficulty; it is a problem – to put it mildly – if a theory allows the able-bodied residents of a place to forcibly expel the handicapped. If, in contrast, Pevnick wants those individuals to be equal to other individuals in their property rights over that society's political institutions, simply in virtue of the fact that they are currently here, then it appears that his argument now reduces to something very much like: we can exclude outsiders because we are here, subject to the law, and they are not. That statement, while true descriptively, is not sufficient as a free-standing justification of the right to exclude.

I am, therefore, unsure that the right way to think about the right to exclude will make reference to the idea of property rights. I believe Pevnick is right about a very great deal; those who are currently members of a political society are rightly able to use their relationship to one another, and to that society's political institutions, as the ground of a right to exclude. I therefore agree with Pevnick – and with Wellman – that we ought to look at what is shared by only fellow members, in our justification of exclusion. On my view, though, what is shared is not best understood in terms of historical property acquisition, nor through the idea of associative freedom. Those who are members of the same society share liability to the same network of legal rights and obligations; we ought to focus on that, in our analysis of the right to exclude.

3.   The jurisdictional theory of exclusion

I have, elsewhere, tried to outline a theory of what provides a legitimate state with the right to exclude (Blake 2013, see also Blake 2003). I will, in the present context, provide a sort of summary of this view. I should repeat, at the start, that I do not think the view can justify anything like the practices of exclusion currently undertaken by wealthy societies. As I have said, to defend the right to exclude is not to defend the status quo. What I want to do is to defend what a justifiable policy of exclusion would have to do to be justified; I do not want to say that any current pattern of exclusion is, in fact, justifiable.

I would begin by noting a simple fact about human rights protection. Human rights are conventionally understood to impose three distinct sorts of obligation on states: to *respect*, to *protect,* and to *fulfill* the specific rights described in human rights instruments. States are prohibited from violating these rights, that is, but they are also obligated to protect the rights of individual persons from being violated by others – and they are obligated to set up instruments designed to provide tools by which rights-violators might be brought to justice. What I want to talk about now is not the content of human rights, but the structure involved in this three-part distinction. The first obligation – respect – is universal in scope; a state may not violate human rights, anywhere in the world. It is no defense against human rights violation that the abused is not a citizen. The second and third obligations, in contrast, are decidedly local, and their localism is defined primarily in territorial terms; states are authorized to defend the human rights of all those who are found within a particular part of the world's surface. This fact is not an accidental feature; it is, instead, built into the system of human rights protection itself that each state will be primarily responsible for the protection of the human rights of only part of the world. Even the International Criminal Court – the most robust instrument of international human rights protection now existing – is prohibited from acting to protect or fulfill human rights in those jurisdictions ruled by governments able and willing to do the job themselves (Rome Statute 1999).

The reason all this is important, I think, is because it shows us what is at stake when someone crosses the territorial border of a state. What matters is not that the person has entered into a new social community; what matters, instead, is that the person has entered into a new legal relationship – one that obligates the current members of that society to defend the rights of that person, by upholding and supporting those rights through legal and political institutions. If there is a right to exclude, I believe these are the materials that will ground it.

How, though, can these materials give rise to a right to exclude? The answer, I think, comes about when we imagine a world in which all human rights are adequately protected. In this imagined world, all citizens have their rights – whatever those might be – adequately respected, protected, and fulfilled. Each society does its job, and every person is provided the space within which their most basic human needs and interests are adequately defended. Imagine, then, that someone wants to move *between* societies. What this person is seeking is a new relationship of rights-protection – one in which a new state, and hence new persons, will bear the burden of protecting that individual's basic rights. Would the state to which he seeks admission have an obligation to admit him? I fail to see why it would; his rights are adequately protected in his own society, by hypothesis, and he is proposing to burden that society's citizens with the obligation to act as the protecting agent to whom all his future claims will be addressed. The state may obtain a limited right to exclude, I believe, when its citizens are able to simply say that they do not want to enter into such a relationship of obligation. There is, I think, a limited right to be free from having to become obligated to others; while we would be morally praiseworthy – indeed, saintly – if we choose to accept all those who sought to enter into such a relationship with us, we seem to be within our rights to refuse to act in defense of those who are already adequately defended.

All this depends, of course, on the plausibility of the principle that we have some limited right to refuse to undertake responsibility for others' rights, when those rights are already adequately protected. I believe a plausible notion of what we owe to one another would make room for such a principle; we seem to have some right to refuse to become obligated – and, indeed, some limited right to use coercion to prevent ourselves from *becoming* so obligated. Think, here, of a repurposed version of Judith Jarvis Thomson's (1971) violinist example. Imagine that violinists require the blood of a healthy person to live. Imagine, further, that they can successfully oblige bystanders to provide that blood simply by latching on; contrary to Thomson's own argument, we might imagine that there is no right to detach the violinist once he is attached. Imagine, finally, that the violinist is already adequately protected by someone else – but he desires to be protected *by you*. Do you have the right to say no? I believe you do; whatever it is that the violinist is entitled to, he is by hypothesis already getting it. He has a right to be protected by someone, but not a right to be protected by the person of his choosing. I believe you can refuse him; I believe you can use some proportional amount of coercion to prevent his alighting upon you. By analogy, we can imagine someone who – like me – emigrated from one wealthy Western society to another. When I crossed the line in the world that describes the American jurisdiction, I created a pattern of obligation on the part of current American citizens – to defend my rights, to protect them, to give me a place within which to speak in their defense, and so on. I believe that these facts gave the United States sufficient reason to exclude me. I am grateful they did not, of course. But I cannot avoid the conclusion that they had every right to keep me out, if they did not want to become so obliged.

There are, of course, any number of worries and difficulties here, none of which I can satisfactorily answer in the present context. I would note that much will turn upon the question of when we are, in fact, obliged to become obliged – obliged, that is, to enter into moral relations with others, in virtue of the deprivation they face abroad. (I would note, further, that everything I say here depends upon the idea that the set of human rights we are entitled to have defended does not include a right to migrate to any country one might wish; if that right were defensible, the argument I give here is untenable.) I will end this section by noting that the theory I give here – even if it can answer these other worries – is unable to defend the right of the government to exclude would-be immigrants from much of the world. Many immigrants are coming from places where their basic human rights are inadequately defended, at best, by their governments. Those individuals, to continue the metaphor, are violinists looking for their protectors; we have no right to use force to prevent these people from obtaining adequate protection by entering into our society. To do that would be to use force to perpetuate someone's morally impermissible status – which, I take it, is itself a morally impermissible act. The right to exclude I defend, in sum, is a rather weak one. I do not think this is a flaw; indeed, I have to say it seems rather correct to think that wealthy states cannot legitimately close their borders to refugees, the starving, and those whose rights have been violated.

I want to end, though, by noting three things that the theory I provide here cannot do – or, rather, cannot do without a great deal of additional thought, none of which I have provided here. There are, as I have said, many questions that are worth asking about the morality of immigration. I will finish here by asking three. The first relates to what moral claims we might make, apart from human rights claims. I understand human rights as instruments designed to protect persons against certain standard threats; threats that can be understood as making lives intolerable generally. What if, though, what makes your life intolerable is the result of something special – something relating to your own particular identity – rather than something widely shared? Imagine, for example, that I have a ground project requiring me to migrate elsewhere in the world; I need to make a religious pilgrimage abroad, or travel to a new country because I have fallen in love with a foreign citizen, or to leave a landlocked society because I yearn to be an oceanographer. All of these might, indeed, be pressing concerns; are they sufficient to generate a right to migration? On a standard human rights model, I think the answer is no; we have a human right to freedom of religion, but that right does not extend to a right to insist that others bear the burdens of our religious practice. I am inclined therefore to think that we might be justly held accountable for limiting our ground projects to those available to us within our own society. The other side, though, is not obviously wrong; we have reason to think that such projects are at the heart of what makes life worth living from the inside (Owen 2010). The answer to this question, I think, will inform a great deal of what current immigration law actually controls: not simply refugee law, but family reunification, professional migration, and perhaps even tourism.

The second question I want to note is the vexed question of the undocumented. If I am right, some of those who want to enter into a particular society may be legitimately refused admission. What of those who, nonetheless, have crossed the border? Are we morally bound to admit them to permanent residence? I have elsewhere suggested that the answer is no; we might be morally disreputable for refusing to admit long-term undocumented citizens into permanent residency, but we do not treat them unjustly by refusing to do so (Blake 2012b). I still believe this to be correct, at least as regards migrants coming from legitimate rights-protecting states; I do, however, want to recognize that there are an enormous number of moral questions we might ask here, none of which are directly addressed in the theory I provide above. We might ask, for example, whether or not the exploitation of the undocumented provides us with an independent reason to provide them with the right to stay (Reed-Sandoval 2014). We might ask, further, whether or not there are particular migrants whose lives would be now so destroyed by deportation that such deportation would now constitute a form of human rights deprivation. We have need, in sum, to ask some very difficult questions about very particular forms of migration; the theory I provide here cannot, on its own, provide us with the answers we need.

The final question I want to ask is the most dangerous of all. It asks, quite simply, whether or not there might be a limit to the amount of diversity present societies can in fact accept. I have already indicated that modern societies can accept a great deal of diversity; Miami is hardly the only case I might have chosen to make this case. That said, it might also be true that there is a limit to the capacity of current members of a society to *accept* diversity. In this argument, I do not mean to defend the idea that the local community is a source of value; I have in mind something rather more sinister than that. I simply mean to note that democracies can be undermined by a simple refusal, on the part of a sufficient number of citizens, to do the jobs required by democratic life – to sacrifice for the common good, to voluntarily pay taxes, to take the law as authoritative, and so on. What should we do if, as it turns out, there is a limit to the amount of linguistic, cultural, or racial diversity that is acceptable to the current membership of a given society? The Constitution, it is said, is not a suicide pact, and neither is liberal democracy; there is no good in holding fast in the name of diversity if it causes the annihilation of democratic practice. But neither is it palatable to limit immigration simply because those who are already here are willing to act upon malign preferences. There is, I think, no particular good answer to this dilemma – and it may become rather pressing for many countries in the coming years, as countries sending migrants abroad may be culturally and ethnically unlike the countries receiving them (Last 2013). Again, I do not think the ideas I have presented here are able to solve the problem; the problem may be one that cannot, without a great deal of work – philosophical and otherwise – be solved at all.

I have, in what has gone before, tried to show that the theory of exclusion I have developed must be supplemented. This is, I think, appropriate in an issue of a journal devoted to new directions in immigration. I would close, though, by reiterating that I take the theory of exclusion I have developed here to be, at worst, incomplete. I believe the best version of the right to exclude we might develop is one that, at its heart, relies upon the moral right to be free from unwanted relationships of obligation – where we have no independent obligation to *become* so obligated. If this produces a vision of the right to exclude that is not capacious, that is perhaps not to be regretted. States, on my view, can indeed engage in the practice of exclusion; the specific policies and practices they develop, though, must respect the rights of all persons to have their human rights adequately protected. States may be allowed to exclude, but they cannot exclude very much.

References

Abizadeh, A., 2008. Democratic theory and border coercion: no right to unilaterally control your own borders. *Political theory*, 36, 37–65.

Blake, M., 2003. Immigration. *In*: R.G. Frey and C.H. Wellman, eds. *A companion to applied ethics*. London: Blackwell, 224–237.

Blake, M., 2012a. Immigration, association, and anti-discrimination. *Ethics*, 122, 1–13.

Blake, M., 2012b. Equality without documents. *In*: C. MacLeod, ed. *Justice and equality*. Calgary: University of Calgary Press, 99–122.

Blake, M., 2012c. Global distributive justice: why political philosophy needs political science. *Annual review of political science*, 15, 121–136.

Blake, M., 2013. Immigration, jurisdiction, and exclusion. *Philosophy and public affairs*, 41, 103–130.

Blake M. and Brock, G., forthcoming. *Debating brain drain: do states have the right to restrict emigration?* Oxford: Oxford University Press.

Carens, J., 1987. Aliens and citizens: the case for open borders. *The review of politics*, 49, 251–273.

Carens, J., 1992. Migration and morality: a liberal Egalitarian perspective. *In*: B. Barry and R.E. Goodin, eds. *Free movement: ethical issues in the transnational migration of people and money*. University Park, PA: Pennsylvania State University Press, 25–47.

Cole, P., 2000. *Philosophies of exclusion*. Edinburgh: Edinburgh University Press.

Collier, P., 2008. *The bottom billion*. Oxford: Oxford University Press.

Easterly, W., 2001. *The elusive quest for growth*. Cambridge, MA: MIT Press.

Ehrenfreund, N., 2007. *The Nuremberg legacy: how the Nazi war crimes trials changed the course of history*. New York: Palgrave MacMillan.

Hosein, A., 2013. Immigration and freedom of movement. *Ethics and global politics*, 6, 25–37.

Huemer, M., 2010. Is there a right to immigrate? *Social theory and practice*, 36, 429–461.

Kapur, D. and McHale, J., 2005. *Give us your best and brightest: the global hunt for talent and its impact on the developing world*. Washington, DC: Center for Global Development.

Kymlicka, W., 1996. *Multicultural citizenship*. Oxford: Oxford University Press.

Last, J., 2013. *What to expect when no one's expecting: America's coming demographic disaster*. New York, NY: Encounter Books.

Miller, D., 2005. Immigration: the case for limits. *In*: A.I. Cohen and C.H. Wellman, eds. *Contemporary debates in applied ethics*. Oxford: Blackwell, 193–206.

Miller, D., 2007. *National responsibility and global justice*. Oxford: Oxford University Press.

Oberman, K., 2011. Immigration, global poverty, and the right to stay. *Political studies*, 59, 253–268.

Owen, D., 2010. National responsibility, global justice, and transnational power. *Review of international studies*, 36, 97–112.

Pevnick, R., 2011. *Immigration and the constraints of justice*. Cambridge: Cambridge University Press.

Pogge, T., 2006. Migration and poverty. *In*: Robert Goodin and Philip Pettit, eds. *Contemporary political philosophy: an anthology*. 2nd ed. Oxford: Blackwell, 710–720.

Pritchett, L., 2006. *Let their people come: breaking the gridlock on global mobility*. Washington, DC: Center for Global Development.

Reed-Sandoval, A., 2014. *Immigrant exploitation and social justice*. Unpublished dissertation.

Rome Statute of the International Criminal Court, 1999. Available from: http://www.un.org/law/icc/index.html.

Song, S., forthcoming. Why do states have the right to control immigration? *NOMOS LVI: immigration*.

Stilz, A., 2010. *Liberal loyalty*. Princeton, NJ: Princeton University Press.

Tamir, Y., 1993. *Liberal nationalism*. Princeton, NJ: Princeton University Press.

Thomson, J., 1971. A defense of abortion. *Philosophy and public affairs*, 1, 47–66.

Torpey, J., 2007. Leaving: a comparative view. *In*: N. Green and F. Weil, eds. *Citizenship and those who leave: the politics of emigration and expatriation*. Urbana, IL: University of Chicago Press, 13–32.

United States Census, 2000. Available from: http://www.mla.org/map_data.

Von Braun J. and Meizen-Dick R., 2009. 'Land-Grabbing' by foreign investors in developing countries: risks and opportunities. IFPRI policy brief 13. Available from: http://www.ifpri.org/sites/default/files/publications/bp013all.pdf.

Walzer, M., 1983. *Spheres of justice*. New York: Basic Books.

Wellman, C.H. and Cole, P., 2011. *Debating the ethics of immigration: is there a right to exclude?* Oxford: Oxford University Press.

Wenar, L., 2008. Property rights and the resource curse. *Philosophy and public affairs*, 36, 2–32.

Wilcox, S., 2009. The open borders debate on immigration. *Philosophy compass*, 4, 1–9.

Ypi, L., 2008. Justice in migration: a closed border Utopia? *Journal of political philosophy*, 16, 391–418.

An overview of the ethics of immigration

Joseph H. Carens*

Department of Political Science, University of Toronto, Toronto, Canada

This essay discusses the ethical issues raised by immigration to rich democratic states in Europe and North America. The article identifies questions about the following topics: access to citizenship, inclusion, residents, temporary workers, irregular migrants, non-discrimination in admissions, family reunification, refugees, and open borders. It explores the answers to these questions that flow from a commitment to democratic principles.

What are the ethical issues raised by immigration? How does immigration affect our understanding of democracy and citizenship? I explore these questions in the context of three presuppositions. First, I am concerned primarily with immigration into the rich democratic states of Europe and North America. I leave open the question of the extent to which this analysis extends to other states.

Second, I presuppose a commitment to democratic principles. That requires an interpretation of democratic principles, and my interpretation can be contested, but I do not pretend that my arguments will have any purchase for those who reject democratic principles altogether. I use the term 'democratic principles' in a very general sense to refer to the broad moral commitments that undergird and justify contemporary political institutions and policies throughout North America and Europe – things like the ideas that all human beings are of equal moral worth, that disagreements should normally be resolved through the principle of majority rule, that we have a duty to respect the rights and freedoms of individuals, that legitimate government depends upon the consent of the governed, that all citizens should be equal under the law, that coercion should only be exercised in accordance with the rule of law,

A slightly different version of this article was recently published as Immigration and Citizenship. *In:* Francisco Gonzalez, ed., *Values and Ethics for the 21st Century.* Madrid: BBVA 2012. pp. 121–164. This article summarizes arguments developed in much more detail in other writings, especially in a recent book (Carens 2013). Because it is an overview, the account provided here is necessarily schematic and cannot consider a host of reasonable objections. I have tried to discuss such challenges in the book.

that people should not be subject to discrimination on the basis of characteristics like race, religion, or gender, that we should respect norms like fairness and reciprocity in our policies, and so on. These ideas can be interpreted in many different ways, and they can even conflict with one another. Nevertheless, on a wide range of topics, like the question of whether it is morally acceptable to force someone to convert from one religion to another, there is no serious disagreement among those who think of themselves as democrats. Many of the questions raised by immigration are interconnected, and a commitment to democratic principles greatly constrains the kinds of answers we can offer to these questions.

Third, for most of my analysis, I am simply going to assume that states normally have a moral right to exercise considerable discretionary control over immigration. I will call this the conventional view. Most of the normative claims that I advance in this article qualify the conventional view but do not challenge it in a fundamental way. At the end of the article, however, I want to step back and offer a fundamental challenge to the conventional view.

I take up the following topics: access to citizenship, inclusion, residents, temporary workers, irregular migrants, non-discrimination in admissions, family reunification, refugees, and, in the final section, open borders. I begin, however, with an objection that would render the rest of the discussion pointless if it were sound.

Sovereignty and self-determination

Some people think that it is a mistake even to talk about the ethics of immigration. Immigration and citizenship should be seen as political issues, not moral ones, they say (Hailbronner 1989). On this view, respect for state sovereignty and democratic self-determination preclude any moral assessments of a state's immigration and citizenship policies.

This sort of attempt to shield immigration and citizenship policies from moral scrutiny is misguided. Consider some examples of past policies that almost everyone today would regard as unjust: the Chinese Exclusion Act of the late nineteenth century that barred people of Chinese descent from naturalization in the United States; the denaturalization policies adopted in the 1930s by many European states (including Germany's infamous Nuremberg Laws); and Canadian and Australian policies of excluding potential immigrants on the basis of race.

To criticize such policies as morally wrong does not entail a rejection of state sovereignty or democratic self-determination. We should distinguish the question of who ought to have the authority to determine a policy from the question of whether a given policy is morally acceptable. We can think that an agent has the moral right to make a decision and still think that the decision itself is morally wrong. That applies just as much to a collective agent like a democratic state as it does to individuals. Moral criticism of the Chinese

Exclusion Act or the Nuremberg Laws or the White Australia Policy does not imply that some other state should have intervened to change those policies or that there should be an overarching authority to compel states to act morally.

The claim that something is a human right or a moral obligation says nothing about how that right or obligation is to be enforced. In fact, in the world today where human rights have come to play an important role, most human rights claims are enforced by states against themselves. That is, states themselves are expected to (and often do) limit their own actions and policies in accordance with human rights norms that they recognize and respect. The very idea of constitutional democracy is built upon the notion of self-limiting government, i.e. that states have the capacity to restrict the exercise of their power in accordance with their norms and values. That is the framework within which I am pursuing the discussion of immigration and citizenship in this article.

Access to citizenship

Who should be granted citizenship and why? I propose the following principles. Anyone born in a state with a reasonable prospect of living there for an extended period should acquire citizenship at birth. Anyone raised in a state for an extended part of her formative years should acquire citizenship automatically over time (or, at the least, acquire an absolute and unqualified right to citizenship). Anyone who comes to a society as an adult immigrant and lives there legally for an extended period ought to acquire a legal right to naturalization – ideally with no further requirements but at most upon meeting certain modest standards regarding language acquisition and knowledge of the receiving society. Finally, people should normally be allowed to acquire dual or even multiple citizenships when they have a genuine connection to the states in question. A democratic state should not make renunciation of other citizenships a requirement for access to its own citizenship whether its citizenship is acquired at birth or through naturalization.

To understand why settled immigrants and their descendants have a moral right to citizenship, we have to think about why the descendants of citizens have a moral claim to citizenship. Consider what we might call the normal case: children who are born to parents who are citizens of the state where their children are born and who live in that state as well. In other words, the baby's parents are resident citizens. Every democratic state grants citizenship automatically to such children at birth. It may seem intuitively obvious that this practice makes moral sense, but I want to make the underlying rationale explicit, and that rationale is not self-evident. Birthright citizenship is not a natural phenomenon. It is a political practice, even when it concerns the children of resident citizens. Would it be morally wrong for a democratic state not to grant citizenship at birth to the children of its own resident citizens, and, if so, why?

We are embodied creatures. Most of our activities take place within some physical space. In the modern world, the physical spaces in which people live are organized politically primarily as territories governed by states. The state can and should recognize even a baby as a person and a bearer of rights. Beyond that, the state where she lives inevitably structures, secures, and promotes her relationships with other human beings, including her family, in various ways.

When a baby is born to parents who are resident citizens, it is reasonable to expect that she will grow up in that state and receive her social formation there and that her life chances and choices will be affected in central ways by that state's laws and policies. She cannot exercise political agency at birth, but she will be able to do so as an adult. If she is to play that role properly, she should see herself prospectively in it as she is growing up. She needs to know that she is entitled to a voice in the community where she lives and that her voice will matter. In addition, political communities are an important source of identity for many, perhaps most, people in the modern world. A baby born to resident citizens is likely to develop a strong sense of identification with the political community in which she lives and in which her parents are citizens. She is likely to see herself and be seen by others as someone who belongs in that community. All of these circumstances shape her relationship with the state where she is born from the outset. They give her a fundamental interest in being recognized immediately as a member of the political community. Granting her citizenship at birth is a way of recognizing that relationship and giving it legal backing.

If you accept the rationale just offered for birthright citizenship for the children of resident citizens, you can see why that practice makes moral sense, indeed why it is morally required of democratic states, given the way the world is organized politically today. But the same rationale applies, for the most part, to a child of immigrants who is born in a state where her parents have settled permanently. She, too, is likely to grow up in the state, to receive her social formation there, and to have her life chances and choices deeply affected by the state's policies. If these are reasons why the children of resident citizens should get citizenship at birth, they are also reasons why the children of settled immigrants should get citizenship at birth. So, too, with the cultivation of political agency, the child of immigrants should be taught from the beginning that she is entitled to a voice in the community where she lives and that her voice will matter. And so, too, with political identity. Like the child of resident citizens, the child of immigrants has a deep interest in seeing herself and in being seen by others as someone who belongs in the political community in which she lives.

Settled immigrants may leave, returning to their country of origin or going elsewhere and taking their children with them, but that is also true of resident citizens. This possibility does not provide a good enough reason to treat the child's membership in the political community as a contingent matter.

Finally, what about the issue of dual citizenship? Does the fact that the children of immigrants get their parents' citizenship at birth provide a democratic state any grounds for denying the children citizenship in the state where they are born and where their parents live?

No, for two reasons. First, citizenship in the country of origin of one's parents is not an adequate substitute for citizenship in the country where one lives. The most important civic relationship a person has is the one with the state where she lives. Second, dual citizenship is now widespread, unavoidable, and generally accepted for children with only one parent who is a resident citizen. More and more children have parents with different nationalities and inherit citizenship status from each of them. It is no longer plausible to claim that this creates any serious practical or principled problems. If dual citizenship is acceptable for children with only one resident citizen parent, it should be acceptable for the children of immigrants as well.

In sum, the most important circumstances shaping a child's relationship with the state from the outset are the same for the child of immigrants as they are for the child of resident citizens. So, the child of immigrants has the same sort of fundamental interest in being recognized immediately and permanently as a member of the political community.

Now consider immigrants who arrive as young children. From both a sociological and a moral perspective, these children are very much like the children born in the state to immigrant parents. They belong, and that belonging should be recognized by making them citizens.

All of the reasons why children should get citizenship as a birthright if they are born in a state after their parents have settled there are also reasons why children who settle in a state at a young age should acquire that state's citizenship. The state where an immigrant child lives profoundly shapes her socialization, her education, her life chances, her identity, and her opportunities for political agency. Her possession of citizenship in another state is not a good reason for denying her citizenship in the state where she lives, and for reasons we have just seen in the discussion of dual citizenship, there is no good reason to require her to give up any other citizenship as a condition of gaining citizenship in the place where she lives. The state where she lives is her home. She has a profound interest in seeing herself and in being seen by others as a member of that political community, and the state has a duty to respect that interest because it has admitted her. The state's grant of citizenship to immigrants who arrive as young children should be unconditional and automatic, just as birthright citizenship is for the children of resident citizens and settled immigrants.

Finally, what about immigrants who arrive as adults? The moral claims that adult immigrants have to citizenship rest on two distinct but related foundations: social membership and democratic legitimacy (Baubock 1994, Rubio-Marín 2000). Their moral claims to citizenship on the basis of social membership are similar in many respects to the moral claims that their children have, namely that human beings become members of a society over time. Immigrants who arrive in a state as adults have received their social formation elsewhere. For that reason, they do not have quite as obvious a claim to be members of the community as their children who grow up within the state and who may even be born there. Nevertheless, living in a community also makes people members. As adult immigrants settle into their new home, they become involved in a dense network of social associations. They acquire interests and identities that are tied up with other members of the society. Their choices and life chances, like those of their children, become shaped by the state's laws and policies. The longer they live there, the stronger their claims to social membership become. At some point, a threshold is passed. They have been there long enough that they simply are members of the community with a strong moral claim to have that membership officially recognized by the state by its granting of citizenship, or at least a right to citizenship if they want it.

The principles of democratic legitimacy give rise to a second basis for adult immigrants to assert a moral claim to citizenship. It is a fundamental democratic principle that everyone should be able to participate in shaping the laws by which she is to be governed and in choosing the representatives who actually make the laws, once she has reached an age where she is able to exercise independent agency. Full voting rights and the right to seek high public office are normally reserved for citizens, and I will simply assume that practice here. Therefore, to meet the requirements of democratic legitimacy, every adult who lives in a democratic political community on an ongoing basis should be a citizen, or, at the least, should have the right to become a citizen if she chooses to do so. Prior to this point, I have not emphasized the democratic legitimacy argument because I have been talking about the citizenship claims of young children who are not old enough to vote or to participate formally in politics, though they have the same sort of claim prospectively as it were, and the democratic legitimacy argument would apply to them if they reached adulthood without receiving citizenship.

Inclusion

Even if immigrants and their descendants have appropriate access to the legal status of citizenship, they can still be marginalized economically, socially, and politically. If citizens of immigrant origin are excluded from the economic and educational opportunities that others enjoy, if they are viewed with suspicion and hostility by their fellow citizens, if their concerns are ignored and their voices not heard in political life, they are not really included in the political community. They may be citizens in a formal sense but they are not really citizens in a fuller, more meaningful sense of the term. They are not likely to see themselves or be seen by others as genuine members of the community. In many important ways, they will not belong.

That is clearly wrong from a democratic perspective. No one thinks that democratic equality requires citizens to be equal in every respect, but the democratic ideal of equal citizenship clearly entails much more than the formal equality of equal legal rights. It requires a commitment to some sort of genuine equality of opportunity in economic life and in education, to freedom from domination in social and political life, to an ethos of mutual respect, compromise, and fairness. Democratic theorists have long worried about the tyranny of majorities over minorities in democracies. Citizens of immigrant origin are one important sort of vulnerable minority. So, democratic principles require the substantive, not merely formal, inclusion of citizens of immigrant origin.

What would substantive inclusion entail? Social scientists who study immigration empirically spend a lot of time trying to figure out what makes for the successful inclusion of immigrants, and especially what sorts of public policies can aid in this process. In conducting these studies, they usually deploy, implicitly or explicitly, a normative standard of proportional equality. That is, they compare how well immigrants and their descendants do on various indicators of well-being and success in economic, social, and political life (e.g. education, economic achievement, social acceptance, and political participation) with how well the rest of the population is doing. The general expectation (again often implicit) is that immigrants themselves should not lag too far behind the rest of the population on these indices and that the descendants of immigrants should do pretty much as well as those whose ancestors have been here longer. If this expectation is not met, then there is a puzzle that needs to be explained through social scientific analysis and perhaps a problem that needs to be addressed through social policy.

Explaining why citizens of immigrant origin are not fully included and what policies might remedy that failure are tasks for empirical researchers. What political philosophers can do is to show how democratic principles guide and limit the policies that states may use to promote the inclusion of citizens of immigrant origin. One important constraint is that democratic states cannot demand social and cultural assimilation as a prerequisite for inclusion. For example, everyone recognizes that a democratic state cannot require its citizens to adopt the religious views of the majority, even if religious differences are a source of social friction. In a contemporary democracy, people have to live with profound differences and to build a shared political community in a context of social and cultural pluralism.

The deep connection between democratic principles and respect for difference is one reason why pronouncements about the 'death of multiculturalism' seem so inappropriate from an ethical perspective. Multiculturalism is a term that can be used in many different ways, but often the social, cultural, and religious diversity that people attribute to multiculturalism is simply the unavoidable consequence of respecting the individual rights and freedoms that democratic states are supposed to provide to all their members (such as rights to religious freedom and rights to live one's life as one chooses so long as one is not harming others). It is dismaying how often contemporary democratic states are willing to override their own principles out of fear and anxiety about differences of culture and identity, as, for example, in the banning of various forms of religious dress and religious architecture.

Democratic justice requires even more than respect for individual rights, however. To achieve justice, it is necessary to pay attention to the ways in which laws and practices may implicitly privilege some over others and to be willing to treat all citizens fairly, even those who are a minority. That will sometimes entail accommodations of various sorts for citizens of immigrant origin and even public recognition of and support for their culture and their identity. It also involves the creation of a public culture in which citizens of immigrant origin are recognized as full members of society and treated with respect. What is at issue here is the way people behave, especially public officials but also ordinary citizens. The value of legal citizenship and formal equality is greatly reduced if the representatives of the state and the rest of the citizenry treat immigrants as outsiders who do not really belong and who have somehow acquired a status that is undeserved.

Immigrants bring change with them. That is inevitable. It is not grounds for constructing the immigrants as a threat or a problem. What is needed instead is some sort of mutual adaptation between citizens of immigrant origin and the majority in the state where the immigrants have settled.

This mutual adaptation will inevitably be asymmetrical. Citizens with deep roots in the society are always in the majority, and that matters in a democracy. They have a legitimate interest in maintaining most of the established institutions and practices. Formal and informal norms are pervasive in any complex modern society. They are often an important kind of collective good, making it possible for people to coordinate their activities without direct supervision or instruction. Most of these formal and informal norms do not conflict with individual rights and freedoms or with the legitimate claims of minorities. To a considerable extent, it is reasonable to expect that citizens of immigrant origin will learn how things work in the receiving society and reasonable to expect that they will conform to these formal and informal norms. This applies even more to their children. The children of immigrants grow up in the state to which their parents have moved. As we have seen, they should grow up as citizens, and, if the educational system functions properly, they should acquire all of the social tools required to function effectively in the society, including mastery of the official language and many other social capacities as well. This does not mean, however, that the children of immigrants can be expected to be like the children of the majority in every respect or that the immigrants themselves have to conform to every established practice.

It is not reasonable to insist that nothing change as a result of immigration. The distinctive experiences, values, and concerns of the immigrants are relevant to an evaluation of the society's formal and informal norms. The way things are done in a society may reflect unconscious and unnecessary elements that come to light only when they are confronted by people who object to them. If citizens of immigrant origin have reasons for wanting things to be done differently, they deserve a hearing and their interests must be considered. Sometimes practices can be changed without any real loss to anyone else beyond the adjustment to the change. Sometimes it may be appropriate to leave existing rules or practices in place and provide exemptions for immigrants. Instead of pretending that the social order is culturally neutral or that it is acceptable to expect citizens of immigrant origin simply to conform to the majority, what is needed is what I have called elsewhere a conception of justice as evenhandedness, i.e. a sensitive balancing of considerations that takes the interests of citizens of immigrant origin seriously and gives them weight without assuming that those interests will always prevail (Carens 2000).

Legal residents

So far I have focussed on access to citizenship and on the inclusion of people of immigrant origin who have become citizens. How should immigrants be treated before they have been settled long enough to become entitled to citizenship?

Let's start with legal residents, i.e. immigrants who have been admitted on an ongoing basis but who have not yet acquired citizenship (whether they are eligible for it or not). Democratic justice greatly constrains the legal distinctions that can be drawn between citizens and residents. Once people have been settled for an extended period, they are morally entitled to the same civil, economic, and social rights as citizens. In a democratic state, these immigrants should enjoy all of the rights that citizens enjoy, except perhaps for the right to vote, the right to hold high public office, and the right to hold high policy-making positions.

This is not such a radical claim as it might sound. With a few significant qualifications, permanent residents do generally enjoy these legal rights in Europe and North America. But why should they?

One answer is that democratic states have an obligation to protect the basic human rights of everyone subject to their jurisdiction. The claim is true as far as it goes, but it does not go far enough. Even tourists and visitors are entitled to protection of their basic human rights, but immigrants with legal residence status have many rights that visitors do not possess. Indeed, if we were to place visitors, residents, and citizens as three categories along a continuum as holders of legal rights, the biggest gap would not be between citizens and residents but between residents and visitors, i.e. not between citizens and non-citizens but between two different kinds of non-citizens. Most of the legal rights created by modern democratic states are neither rights granted to everyone present nor rights possessed only by citizens. Instead, they are rights possessed by both citizens and permanent residents. Let's see why that makes moral sense.

What is it that residents and citizens have in common that is morally significant and makes it justifiable to give them legal rights that are not given to visitors? The answer is obvious. They live in the society. Living there gives them interests that visitors do not have, interests that deserve legal recognition and protection. Living there makes them members of civil society. Someone might object that this is circular, that it begs the question of why the visitors are only visitors. Perhaps they would like to become residents too and are not being allowed to do so. But that is an issue I will consider later. For the moment, I am just assuming the legitimacy of the state's right to decide which non-citizens will become residents and asking how states should treat those to whom it has granted resident status.

Let's start with some of the areas where residents do generally enjoy the same rights as citizens and see why this arrangement makes moral sense. Consider first the right to seek employment. In any society in which acquiring the means to live depends upon gainful employment, denying access to work to people who reside there is like denying access to life itself. It would be contradictory to allow people to live in a society while denying them the means to do so. For the same reasons, to deny residents the kinds of labor rights that other workers enjoy (e.g. the protections provided by health and safety legislation, the right to join unions, etc.) would be to place them at an unfair disadvantage. I know of no one advocating such a course.

If we consider social insurance programs financed by compulsory deductions from workers' pay (old age pensions, unemployment compensation, compensation for workplace accidents, etc.), we can see that it would hardly be reasonable to require people to pay into these programs and then to deny them access to the benefits they provide. The principle of reciprocity on which such programs are based requires that those who pay should be eligible. (Some programs of this sort have minimum periods of employment that must be fulfilled before one can collect, and, of course, it is appropriate to impose the same limits on non-citizens – but not longer ones.) Again, I don't think this principle is seriously contested even if it is sometimes breached in practice.

Finally, consider access to general social programs, such as publicly funded education and health care, provided to the general population. Of course, different states provide different levels of benefits, but one rarely hears arguments for treating legal permanent residents differently from citizens with regard to these programs. The reason why seems obvious. Residents also pay the taxes that fund these programs. Again, an elementary sense of reciprocity makes it clear that excluding residents from the benefits of such general public expenditures would be unjust.

So, for the vast majority of the legal rights that democratic states create, there is no plausible case to be made for distinguishing between residents and citizens, apart from political rights. They are, and ought to be seen as, rights of membership, not rights of citizenship. The debates come at the margins, mainly around security of residence, access to public employment and access to redistributive social programs. I do not have the space to develop the arguments here, but I have argued elsewhere that during the early stages of settlement, it is permissible to limit rights to redistributive benefits and protection against deportation, but that the longer people stay in a society, the stronger their moral claims become to be treated like citizens in these respects as well, even if they remain legal residents (Carens 2002, 2013). In the same places, I have argued that restrictions on access to public employment, except for policy-making or security positions, are always a form of illegitimate discrimination.

Temporary workers

May democratic states admit people to work but only for a limited period? If so, what legal rights should these temporary workers have? In my view, democratic states may admit people to work while limiting the duration of their stay and their access to redistributive social programs, but other sorts of restrictions are morally problematic.

In the previous section, I asserted that a person's moral claims in a society grow over time. That applies to residence as well. The longer someone stays, the stronger her claim to remain becomes. One implication of that principle is that being present for a limited period does not establish a strong claim to remain. So, if a democratic state admits someone to work on a temporary visa and that person has no other moral claim to remain, the state may reasonably require her to leave when her visa expires. However, if the state renews a temporary visa repeatedly, the state is eventually obliged to convert the temporary visa into a permanent one. That follows from the idea that the moral claim to stay grows over time. The European Union has recognized this principle in its recent directive recommending that third country nationals (that is, people from outside the EU) be granted a right of permanent residence if they have been legally residing in an EU state for five years (European Council 2003).

The arguments for granting temporary workers most of the legal rights that citizens and residents possess are based on the commitment of democratic states to general human rights, to the principle of reciprocity, and to whatever standards a state establishes as the minimum morally acceptable conditions of employment within its jurisdiction.

As I noted previously, even visitors and tourists enjoy general human rights, such as security of person and property. So, I will just assume that temporary migrant workers are entitled to those rights as well.

What about other rights? Let's distinguish among three general areas: working conditions (which include things like health and safety regulations and laws regarding minimum wages, overtime pay, and paid holidays and vacations), social programs directly tied to workforce participation, (which include things like unemployment compensation and compulsory pension plans), and other social programs (which include income support programs, health care, education, recreation, and anything else the state spends money on for the benefit of the domestic population).

Temporary migrants should enjoy the same rights with respect to working conditions as citizens and permanent residents. The purpose of those rules and regulations is to set the minimum acceptable working conditions within a particular democratic community based on the understanding of what is acceptable that is generated by the community's internal democratic processes. Temporary migrants are working within the state's jurisdiction. Therefore, the policies that regulate working conditions for citizens and permanent residents should apply to them as well.

What about programs tied to workforce participation? When programs are designed as contributory schemes, the injustice of excluding temporary migrant workers from them is especially obvious. It is blatantly unfair to require people to pay into an insurance scheme if they are not eligible for the benefits. This violates an elementary principle of reciprocity. But the basic principle of including temporary migrant workers in the programs or compensating them for their exclusion does not rest solely on the method by which the program is financed. As long as the rationale of the program is intimately linked to workforce participation, it should include all workers, temporary migrants or not.

Finally, every state provides a wide range of services to those within its territory, including such things as police and fire protection, public education, libraries, recreational facilities, and so on. There is no justification for excluding temporary workers from most of these programs. In practice, the programs from which temporary workers are most likely to be excluded and the ones where the normative justification of the exclusion seem most plausible are programs that are financed by some general tax and that have as their primary goal the transfer of resources from better off members of the community to worse off ones. I have in mind things like income support programs and other programs aimed at poorer members of society such as social housing. I am not suggesting that it would be wrong to include temporary workers in such programs. On the contrary, I think it would be admirable to include them, and some states do. I am simply saying that it is morally permissible to exclude temporary workers from programs that have redistribution as their primary goal. If such programs are not based directly on a contributory principle, excluding recent arrivals from them does not violate the principle of reciprocity. Since the goal of the programs is to support needy members of the community and since the claim to full membership is something that is only gradually acquired, exclusion of recent arrivals does not seem unjust (although it may be ungenerous). Of course, these programs are funded out of general tax revenues and temporary workers also pay taxes, but their claim to participate in a program based on redistributive taxation – taking from better off members of the community to benefit the less well off – is not as powerful as their claim to participate in a program whose benefits are directly tied to the worker's contributions. The moral claims of temporary workers to be able to participate in redistributive programs grow over time, but, as we have seen, so does their claim to permanent, full membership.

Irregular migrants

Now consider immigrants who have settled without authorization, whom I will call irregular migrants. What legal rights, if any, should they have?

Given my initial assumption of the state's right to control immigration, it follows that states are morally entitled to deport irregular migrants if they apprehend them. Nevertheless, I want to claim that irregular migrants should enjoy most of the civil, economic, and social rights that other workers enjoy, and that states should normally create a firewall between the enforcement of immigration laws on the one hand and the protection of the legal rights of irregular migrants on the other so that these rights can be really effective. Furthermore, I argue that over time, irregular migrants acquire a moral right to remain and to have their status regularized.

At first blush, it may appear puzzling to suggest that irregular migrants should have any legal rights. Since they are violating the state's law by settling and working without authorization, why should the state be obliged to grant them any legal rights at all? A moment's reflection, however, makes us aware that irregular migrants are entitled to at least some legal rights. Unlike medieval regimes, modern democratic states do not make criminals into outlaws – people entirely outside the pale of the law's protection. Irregular migrants are clearly entitled to the protection of their basic human rights. The right to security of one's person and property is a good example. The police are supposed to protect even irregular migrants from being robbed and killed. People do not forfeit their right to be secure in their persons and their possessions simply in virtue of being present without authorization. The right to a fair trial and the right to emergency health care are other examples.

The fact that people are legally entitled to certain rights does not mean that they actually are able to make use of those rights. It is a familiar point that irregular migrants are so worried about coming to the attention of the authorities that they are often reluctant to pursue the legal protections and remedies to which they are formally entitled, even when their most basic human rights are at stake. This creates a serious normative problem for democratic states. It makes no moral sense to provide people with purely formal legal rights under conditions that make it impossible for people to exercise those rights effectively.

What is to be done? There is at least a partial solution to this problem. States can and should build a firewall between immigration law enforcement on the one hand and the protection of basic human rights on the other. We ought to establish as a firm legal principle that no information gathered by those responsible for protecting and realizing basic human rights can be used for immigration enforcement purposes. We ought to guarantee that people will be able to pursue their basic rights without exposing themselves to apprehension and deportation. For example, if irregular migrants are victims of a crime or witnesses to one, they should be able to go to the police, report the crime, and serve as witnesses without fear that this will increase the chances of their being apprehended and deported by immigration officials. If they need emergency health care, they should be able to seek help without worrying that the hospital will disclose their identity to those responsible for enforcing immigration laws.

I cannot develop the details here, but roughly the same pattern of argument applies to many other areas of legal rights. The children of irregular migrants should be entitled to a free and compulsory education in the public schools (because that sort of education should be regarded as a basic human right for anyone living within a society). There should be a firewall between the provision of these educational services and the enforcement of immigration laws. Irregular migrants should be legally entitled to their pay if they work and should be legally entitled to the same rights and protections with regard to working conditions as other workers, because these rights and protections reflect a particular democratic state's minimum standards for acceptable working conditions within its territory. Again, these rights can only be effective if they are backed up be a firewall with respect to immigration enforcement.

As the list of rights grows, one might ask whether there are any rights that authorized immigrants have to which the unauthorized immigrants are not entitled. Given the initial assumption about the state's right to control its borders, I would say that irregular migrants are not normally morally entitled to receive the benefits of income support programs, and, of course, they are not morally entitled to stay. Even these constraints are not absolute, however. The longer one stays in a society, the stronger one's claim to membership. That applies even in the case of those who have settled without authorization. When people settle in a country, they form connections and attachments that generate strong moral claims over time. After a while, the conditions of admission become irrelevant.

This recognition of the moral importance of the length of stay, even if unauthorized, is reflected in the practices of many states, both in the granting of general amnesties to unauthorized residents which are almost always limited to those who have already been in the country for an extended period and in the common practice of allowing for exemptions from the normal rules of deportation on compassionate and humanitarian grounds, which in turn are almost always linked to long residence in the country. I do not mean to suggest that everyone accepts this, however. The law almost never recognizes an individual right of unauthorized residents to stay (except occasionally with respect to those who have been present as children). Moreover, many would object to amnesties (whether individual or collective) on the grounds that they reward lawbreaking and encourage more unauthorized immigration. Nevertheless, in my view, long-term settlement does carry moral weight and eventually even grounds a moral right to stay that ought to be recognized in law.

Non-discrimination in admissions

Let me turn now to questions about who should get in. In what ways, if any, is the state's right to control admissions morally constrained? As with citizenship, people sometimes say that control over immigration is a fundamental feature of sovereignty and self-determination and so cannot be subject to any normative constraints external to the community's will. But no one really believes this if pressed. Democracies are not entitled to a moral carte blanche. One obvious constraint on immigration policies is the principle of non-discrimination. No one today would claim that a democratic state could legitimately bar African and Asian immigrants just because of their racial or ethnic origins, though this is precisely what Canada, the United States, and Australia did quite openly in the past. To exclude immigrants on the basis of race or ethnicity is a fundamental violation of democratic principles. The same principle applies to religion. There is no possible justification within a democratic framework for excluding people because of their religion. Today, of course, it is Islam that is the focus of exclusion, though religion is often intertwined here with race and ethnicity. Many people in Europe and North America are afraid of Muslims (as, in years past, they were afraid of Catholics and Jews). Western states know that open discrimination against Muslims is incompatible with their principles, and that is precisely why, if they do seek to exclude Muslim immigrants, they usually try to conceal what they are doing. They do not openly announce these exclusions (as they did in their racially exclusive policies in the past), but find other pretexts and justifications – couched in neutral terms but designed to have particular effects. As the old saying goes, hypocrisy is the tribute that vice pays to virtue.

In addition to not discriminating, there are at least two other important moral limits on the state's right to control immigration and to admit or exclude whomever it wants, even under the conventional view of the state's general right to control immigration. These limits are family reunification and refugees.

Family reunification

Democratic states are morally obliged to admit the immediate family members of citizens and residents. It is worth noting first that family reunification is primarily about the moral claims of insiders, not outsiders. The state's obligation to admit immediate family members is derived not so much from the claims of those seeking to enter as the claims of those they seek to join: citizens or residents or others who have been admitted for an extended period. It is not a question here of a cosmopolitan challenge to the state's control over admissions but rather of the responsibilities of democratic states towards those whom they govern. Democratic states have an obligation to take the vital interests of their own members into account. The whole notion that individual rights set limits to what may be done in the name of the collective rests upon this supposition.

People have a deep and vital interest in being able to live with their immediate family members. No one disputes this. But why must this interest in family life be met by admitting the family members? Could it not be satisfied just as well by the departure of the family member(s) present to join those abroad. Why is the state obliged to shape its admissions policies to suit the locational preferences of individuals?

Note first that if the family members have different citizenships, at least one state must be willing to admit non-citizen close family members if the family is to be able to live together. But the deeper point is that a democratic state should respect the locational preferences of its citizens and residents because people have a deep and vital interest in being able to continue living in a society where they have settled and sunk roots as well as a deep and vital interest in living with their immediate family members. Of course, people sometimes have good reasons of their own to leave and sometimes face circumstances that require them to make painful choices. (If two people from different countries fall in love, they cannot both live in their home countries and live together.) So, people must be free to leave. But no one should be forced by the state to choose between home and family. Whatever the state's general interest in controlling immigration, that interest cannot plausibly be construed to require a complete ban on the admission of non-citizens, and cannot normally be sufficient to justify restrictions on family reunification. I add the qualifier 'normally' because even basic rights are rarely absolute, and the right to family reunification cannot be conceived as absolute. States do not have an obligation to admit people whom they have good reason to regard as a threat to national security, for example, even if they are family members. But the right of people to live with their family clearly sets a moral limit to the state's right simply to set its admissions policy as it chooses. Some special justification is needed to override the claim to family reunification, not merely the usual calculation of state interests.

Most democratic states acknowledge this principle, and that is a major reason why there has been a significant continuing flow of immigrants into Europe even after European states stopped recruiting guest workers. We now see some European states trying to restrict this right at the margins (e.g. Denmark's raising of the marriage age, the French debate over DNA tests, the Dutch insistence that potential family immigrants pass a test before admission, etc.). These restrictions deserve criticism because they conflict with the principle of family reunification, but so far no European state has directly attacked the principle itself, nor could any state do so without abandoning its commitment to democratic principles and human rights.

Finally, the concept of family reunification raises interesting questions about cultural variation in the definition of family. I cannot pursue those issues here, but let me simply assert the proposition that democratic states ought to admit same-sex partners for purposes of family reunification. Some already do this.

Refugees

Now consider refugees. For these purposes, let's just define refugees in broad terms as people forced to flee their home countries with no reasonable prospect of returning there in the foreseeable future. They need new homes. Who should provide those homes? What obligations do we have, if any, to admit refugees?

Note first that my discussion of refugees does not challenge the conventional view about the state's right to exercise discretionary control over immigration under normal circumstances. Rather it presupposes that view. The claim in this section is that refugees are a special case that qualifies the conventional view rather than rejecting it altogether.

In exploring our obligation to admit refugees, let's distinguish between refugees whose plight we are responsible for and refugees whose plight we are not responsible for. Clearly, we have a moral responsibility to find homes and permanent solutions for refugees who have had to flee their homes because of our actions. Americans – whether supporters or opponents of the war – recognized this in the wake of the Vietnam War and took in hundreds of thousands of refugees from Vietnam, Cambodia, and Laos. Americans have the same sort of obligation towards refugees from Iraq and Afghanistan, especially those who have been forced to flee because their lives are in danger as a result of their cooperation with Americans. This issue should have nothing to do with whether one supports or opposes these wars. It is deep moral failure that Americans have done so little in this regard.

All rich countries have responsibilities for refugee flows that we can already foresee. We should already be starting to think about who ought to take in ecological refugees – people forced to flee their homes because of global warming and the resulting changes in their physical environment. Clearly, the rich industrial states bear a major responsibility for the changes that are already taking place. It is our responsibility, not those of geographically proximate states, to find a place for these people to live. Given the divergence between what justice requires and what serves our interests in this case, I am not optimistic about the likelihood of our meeting our responsibilities, but that is no reason not to acknowledge them in a philosophical inquiry like this one.

Even if our own state is not responsible for the circumstances that led a particular group of refugees to flee, we may still have moral obligations to respond to their needs and to offer them a new place to live. The failures of democratic states to respond to the plight of Jews fleeing Hitler is one of the great shames of modern history. The Holocaust was an important part of the impetus behind the creation of the modern refugee regime, a regime that promised that no refugee would be turned away, that refugees would be able to find new homes.

Some will object that many people claim to be refugees when they are really just economic migrants, looking for a better life. There is no doubt that some of the people who seek refugee status, perhaps even many of them, would not qualify under the provisions of the Geneva Convention or other existing refugee legislation. It is also the case, however, that the rich industrial states have systematically tried to prevent everyone who might be able to file a plausible refugee claim from coming. All rich states have imposed visa requirements and carrier sanctions that are entirely indiscriminate in their exclusions (Gibney 2006). When people do arrive seeking protection, they are often met with narrow legal interpretations that deny them refugee status even though officials cannot send them back where they came from because they know that they would be in danger. They wind up in limbo for years. This is a profound moral failure, but I confess that the gap between our interests and our moral duties is so great here that I despair of a feasible solution.

Open borders

Up to this point, I have been exploring the ethics of immigration within the constraints of the conventional view that states are normally entitled to exercise discretionary control over immigration. The last few sections – on irregular migrants, family reunification, and refugees – qualify the conventional view but do not challenge it directly. Now let's explore the possibility of a direct challenge to the conventional view. Why might someone think that a commitment to democratic principles should lead rich states to open their borders much more fully?

Borders have guards and the guards have guns. This is an obvious fact of political life but one that is easily hidden from view – at least from the view of those of us who are citizens of affluent Western democracies. If we see the guards and guns at all, we find them reassuring because we think of them as there to protect us rather than to keep us out. To Africans in small, leaky vessels seeking to avoid patrol boats while they cross the Mediterranean to southern Europe or to Mexicans willing to risk death from heat and exposure in the Arizona desert to evade the fences and border patrols, it is quite different. To these people, the borders, guards, and guns are all too apparent, their goal of exclusion all too real. What justifies the use of force against such people? Perhaps borders and guards can be justified as a way of keeping out terrorists, armed invaders, or criminals. But most of those trying to get in are not like that. They are ordinary, peaceful people, seeking only the opportunity to build decent, secure lives for themselves and their families. On what moral grounds can we keep out these sorts of people? What gives anyone the right to point guns at them?

To most people, the answer to this question will seem obvious. The power to admit or exclude non-citizens is inherent in sovereignty and essential for any political community. Every state has the legal and moral right to exercise that right in pursuit of its own national interest and of the common good of the members of its community, even if that means denying entry to peaceful, needy foreigners. States may choose to be generous in admitting immigrants, but, in most cases at least, they are under no obligation to do so.

I want to challenge that view. In principle, I argue, borders should generally be open and people should normally be free to leave their country of origin and settle in another, subject only to the sorts of constraints that bind current citizens in their new country. The argument is strongest when applied to the migration of people from poor, developing countries to Europe and North America, but it applies more generally.

Citizenship in Western democracies is the modern equivalent of feudal privilege – an inherited status that greatly enhances one's life chances. Like feudal birthright privileges, the privileges that flow from birthright citizenship in Western democracies are hard to justify when one thinks about them closely. To be born a citizen of an affluent state in Europe or North America is like being born into the nobility (even though most of us belong to the lesser nobility). To be born a citizen of a poor country in Asia or Africa is (for most) like being born into the peasantry in the Middle Ages (even if there are a few rich peasants). In this context, limiting entry to the rich states is a way of protecting a birthright privilege. Reformers in the late Middle Ages objected to the way feudalism restricted freedom, including the freedom of individuals to move from one place to another in search of a better life – a constraint that was crucial to the maintenance of the feudal system. But modern practices of citizenship and state control over borders tie people to the land of their birth almost as effectively. If the feudal practices were wrong, what justifies the modern ones?

My starting point is an assumption of human moral equality, a commitment to the equal moral worth of all human beings. This does not entail the sort of cosmopolitanism that requires every agent to consider the interests of all human beings before acting or that insists that every policy or institution be assessed directly in terms of its effects on all human beings. It does, however, entail a commitment to justification through reason-giving and reflection that does not simply presuppose the validity of conventional moral views or the legitimacy of existing arrangements or our entitlement to what we have.

Freedom of movement is both an important liberty in itself and a prerequisite for other freedoms. So, we should start with a presumption for free migration. Restrictions on migration, like any use of force, need to be defended. Nevertheless, freedom of movement is only one important human interest, and it may conflict with others. There is no reason to assume that all important human freedoms are fully compatible with one another or with other basic human interests. Restrictions on particular freedoms may sometimes be justified because they will promote liberty overall or because they will promote other important human concerns, but we cannot justify restrictions on the freedom of others simply by saying that the restrictions are good for us. We have to show that they somehow take everyone's legitimate claims into account, that we are not violating our fundamental commitment to equal moral worth.

A commitment to equal moral worth may not require us to treat people identically in every way, but it does require us to respect basic human freedoms. People should be free to pursue their own projects and to make their own choices about how they live their lives so long as this does not interfere with the legitimate claims of other individuals to do likewise. To enjoy this general sort of freedom, people have to be free to move where they want (subject to the same restraints as others with regard to respect for private property, the use of public property, etc.). The right to go where you want is itself an important human freedom. It is precisely this freedom, and all that this freedom makes possible, that is taken away by imprisonment. Thus, conventional immigration controls improperly limit the freedom of non-citizens who are not threatening the basic rights and freedoms of citizens.

A commitment to equal moral worth requires some sort of basic commitment to equal opportunity. Access to social positions should be determined by an individual's actual talents and capacities, not limited on the basis of arbitrary native characteristics (such as class, race, or sex). But freedom of movement is essential for equality of opportunity. You have to be able to move to where the opportunities are in order to take advantage of them. Again, the conventional pattern of border controls greatly restricts opportunities for potential immigrants.

Finally, a commitment to equal moral worth entails some commitment to the reduction of existing economic, social, and political inequalities, partly as a means of realizing equal freedom and equal opportunity and partly as a desirable end in itself. Freedom of movement would contribute to a reduction of political, social, and economic inequalities. There are millions of people in poor states today who long for the freedom and economic opportunity they could find in Europe and North America. Many of them take great risks to come. If the borders were open, millions more would move. The exclusion of so many poor and desperate people seems hard to justify from a perspective that takes seriously the claims of all individuals as free and equal moral persons.

I have no illusions about the likelihood of rich states actually opening their borders. The primary motivation for this open borders argument is my sense that it is of vital importance to gain a critical perspective on the ways in which our collective choices are constrained, even when we cannot do anything to alter those constraints. Social institutions and practices may be deeply unjust and yet so firmly established that, for all practical purposes, they must be taken as background givens in deciding how to act in the world at a particular moment in time. For example, feudalism and slavery were unjust social arrangements that were deeply entrenched in places in the past. In those contexts, there was no real hope of transcending them in a foreseeable future. Yet, criticism was still appropriate.

Even if we have to take such arrangements as givens for purposes of immediate action in a particular context, we should not forget about our assessment of their fundamental character. Otherwise, we wind up legitimating what should only be endured. Of course, most people in democratic states think that the institutions they inhabit have nothing in common with feudalism and slavery from a normative perspective. The social arrangements of democratic states, they suppose, are just – or nearly so. It is precisely that complacency that the open borders argument is intended to undermine. For I imagine (or at least hope) that in a century or two people will look back upon our world with bafflement or shock. Just as we wonder about the moral blindness of feudal aristocrats and Southern slave owners, future generations may ask themselves how democrats today could have possibly failed to see the deep injustice of a world so starkly divided between haves and have nots and why we felt so complacent about this division, so unwilling to do what we could to change it.

The argument for open borders provides one way of bringing this deep injustice of the modern world into view. It is only a partial perspective, to be sure, because even if borders were open that would not address all of the underlying injustices that make people want to move. But it is a useful perspective because our responsibility for keeping people from immigrating is clear and direct, whereas our responsibility for poverty and oppression elsewhere often is not as obvious, at least to many people. We have to use overt force to prevent people from moving. We need borders with barriers and guards with guns to keep out people whose only goal is to work hard to build a decent life for themselves and their children. And that is something we could change. At the least, we could let many more people in. Our refusal to do so is a choice we make, and one that keeps many of them from having a chance at a decent life.

References

Baubock, R., 1994. *Transnational citizenship: membership and rights in international migration*. Aldershot: Edward Elgar.

Carens, J.H., 2000. *Culture, citizenship, and community: a contextual exploration of justice as evenhandedness*. Oxford: Oxford University Press.

Carens, J.H., 2002. Citizenship and civil society: what rights for residents? *In*: R. Hansen and P. Weil, eds. *Dual nationality, social rights and federal citizenship in the US and Europe: the reinvention of citizenship*. Oxford: Berghahn Books, 100–118.

Carens, J.H., 2013. *The ethics of immigration*. New York: Oxford University Press.

European Council, 2003. European Council Directive 2003/109/EC.

Gibney, M., 2006. A thousand little Guantanamos: western states and measures to prevent the arrival of refugees. *In*: K. Tunstall, ed. *Migration, displacement, asylum: The Oxford Amnesty Lectures 2004*. Oxford: Oxford University Press, 139–160.

Hailbronner, K., 1989. Citizenship and nationhood in Germany. *In*: William Rogers Brubaker, ed. *Immigration and the politics of citizenship in Europe and North America*. Lanham, MD: German Marshall Fund and University Press of America, 67–79.

Rubio-Marín, R., 2000. *Immigration as a democratic challenge*. Cambridge: Cambridge University Press.

Reframing the brain drain

Alex Sager

Department of Philosophy, Portland State University, Portland, OR, USA

Theorists concerned about the distributive effects of skilled emigration ('brain drain') often argue that its harmful effects can be justly mitigated by restricting emigration from sending countries or by limiting immigration opportunities to receiving countries. I raise moral and practical concerns against restricting the movement of skilled migrants and contend that conceptualizing the moral issue in these terms leads theorists to neglect the moral salience of institutions that determine the distributive effects of migration. Using an analogy to skilled migration in a domestic context, I argue for locating brain drain in a more holistic, institutional context that includes the reform of global institutions and of policies affecting migration.

Political theorists concerned with the distributive effects of migration often invoke the potential that 'brain drain' – the emigration of skilled workers – may exacerbate regional inequalities and stunt social and economic development. My goal is to show that when we properly contextualize skilled migration within larger questions of migration and development, we discover that it plays a limited and secondary role within a theory of distributive justice. The normative literature on brain drain usually asks whether it is permissible to impose emigration or immigration restrictions to prevent skilled workers from migrating. This is the wrong question. It unduly isolates skilled migration from the many economic and social structures that determine its effects and prevents normative theorists from considering all of the moral aspects relevant to policy. It also discourages theorists from thinking about skilled migration within the context of more comprehensive migration and development policies. Rather than focusing on the permissibility of migration restrictions for skilled workers, we should ask what institutions must be put in place so that migration will not have harmful effects and interact with other policies to make people better off.

I propose an analysis of the institutions shaping migration flows as the basis for a theory of justice in migration. This analysis asks how migration under certain institutions and practices, including border controls, trade agreements, social and cultural networks, and domestic policies, can contribute to an unjust allocation of benefits and burdens. I contend that if background institutions causally contribute to the systematical disadvantage of some groups and if there are reasonable measures that could mitigate these harms, then moral obligations arise for people upholding these institutions (Pogge 2002). I show how institutions, especially global institutions, systematically shape migration in ways that unjustly disadvantage people around the world. Nonetheless, I contend that practical and normative considerations mitigate against restrictions on the migration of skilled workers. Rather, we need to implement global and national institutional reforms so that migration ceases to be a contributing factor to inequitable distributions.

1. The moral implications of skilled migration

The moral implications of brain drain depend on empirical claims about human capital, development, and the delivery of vital services, and on moral claims about the sources of obligation. Theorists who support policies to mitigate brain drain accept the *empirical* claim that *if fewer skilled migrants had migrated, then some people in the sending country would be better off than they are*. If it turns out that migration almost always has positive or neutral effects for developing regions through remittances, return migration, technology transfer, or by causing people who ultimately choose not to migrate to acquire new skills, then brain drain is a topic of limited normative interest. Pessimists about the effects of skilled migration also make a *moral* claim that the fact that some people in the sending country are worse off entails moral obligations for the emigrants, citizens of receiving countries, and/or officials in sending countries.

One difficulty with the empirical counterfactual is that it is hard to evaluate. The study of skilled migration is beset by methodological, conceptual, and measurement challenges (Sahay 2009, pp. 19–56). Data on skilled migration and remittances are difficult to obtain and to compare across countries (Kapur and McHale 2005, pp. 11–35) and the impact of skilled migration is even less understood. The fear of brain drain rests on the conviction that skilled workers are the people most likely to build and sustain governments, schools, hospitals, and firms that promote development (Kapur and McHale 2005). Workers with scarce, vital skills such as medical training also provide immediate benefits. Beyond contributions to economic development, skilled workers often acquire their education at the expense of their country of origin. For example, a recent study concludes that it cost sub-Saharan African countries suffering from a prevalence of 5% or greater of HIV/AIDS $2 billion to educate doctors who migrated to Australia, Canada, the United Kingdom, and the United States (Mills *et al.* 2011).

But while the migration of skilled workers might reduce growth, lower the tax base, and deprive sending regions of vital skills for development, a cost–benefit analysis needs to consider the effect of remittances, circular and return migration, technological bridges, and the incentive for people to raise overall levels of human capital by investing in education (Docquier and

Abdelslam 2006). This task also raises questions about the scope of justice. Who is included in the calculus of costs and benefits? People left behind? Migrants? Residents of receiving countries? Third-parties from countries outside of migration networks? The weights we assign to different interests – including whether we assign priority to the interests of vulnerable people or to special relationships – will also change our moral assessment.

Migration also interacts with other factors in complex, non-linear ways. Even if we have accurate estimates about the size of remissions, their role in promoting entrepreneurship or the development of human capital is hard to determine. Similarly, it is difficult to estimate gains from return migration and from diaspora connections. Finally, the time horizon considered has conceptual and moral implications. For example, internal migration from rural to urban areas may lead to short-term struggles for people left behind but spur long-term growth. We need to decide about how to calculate, weigh, and allocate present and future harms and benefits.

Partly due to the ambiguity in the empirical literature, much of the philosophical literature on brain drain has emphasized the migration of health care workers from underserved regions in the South. Migration of health workers appears to many to provide an instance where the costs of brain drain sometimes clearly outweigh the benefits (Mullan 2005). Even in this case, there are obstacles to determining the health impacts of skilled migration, to identifying the causal factors that lead people to leave, and to explaining the impact of their emigration. Health workers may migrate in response to unstable, insecure communities and poor, dangerous working conditions (Bueno de Mesquita and Gordon 2005), or to structural changes in the global economy (Van Eyck 2004). If they are leaving because their basic rights are not met in their community, then their personal responsibility and their local government's right to use coercion to discourage their exit is mitigated. Nor can we automatically infer that had skilled workers remained, they would have ameliorated local health crises (Clemens 2007). Quality of health care depends on many other factors, including the overall state of the government and economy. If health care workers are forced to remain under authoritarian regimes with poor infrastructure, they may end up unemployed or working in other sectors and contributing to 'brain waste.'

Moreover, health care workers may be importantly different from other skilled migrants (Bach 2008) and thus of limited relevance to a general theory about the justice of skilled migration. Since health care directly involves questions of life and death, crises in sub-Saharan Africa and other highly vulnerable regions might be considered instances of 'states of emergency' that tell us relatively little about how just institutions should function under normal conditions. This point can be extended to any workers whose presence is needed to address events such as natural disasters or war which permit the temporary suspension of the rule of law and basic rights and freedoms: our conclusions about the justice of restricting the migration of these workers may only tell us about the legitimate suspension of considerations of justice under extreme circumstances, not about what justice normally requires.

Even if emigration sometimes does have harmful effects, this does not automatically establish moral rights or duties. This would only occur if states, communities, vulnerable individuals, and other agents have a legitimate claim on workers' talents. Are states and other actors entitled to coercively distribute scarce human capital (i.e. *individuals* endowed with human capital) so that the resources it generates are fairly distributed? This proposal appears to conflict with widely acknowledged rights such as freedom of occupation and freedom of emigration and with principles of autonomy and self-ownership. Joseph Carens objects that this sort of solution 'proposes to extract benefits for some people by, in effect, imprisoning them' (Carens 1992, p. 33). Fernando Tesón raises a similar objection that identification of human beings as 'highly skilled' (or 'unskilled') units of human capital 'unduly personifies the state as the owner of human capital, just as an investor owns his money, and therefore fails to treat persons as autonomous agents' (Tesón 2008, p. 8). These objections apply most strongly to proposals to restrict emigration and to bonding, but they also emphasize the need for states and for individuals to demonstrate that skilled migrants owe them moral obligations that include forgoing emigration to work in their professions. And even if skilled workers have moral obligations, proponents of coercive measures need to show that these are moral obligations that can be enforced through coercive restrictions of core human freedoms and self-ownership.

In fact, it is possible to question the moral relevance of migration's effects on the allocation of resources. Skilled workers' basic rights could trump distributive concerns and put limits on the justifiable use of state coercion to obligate workers to remain in their territories of birth or to make emigration conditional on the payment of taxes or fees. Individual rights do place significant restraints on the scope of what measures states can justly undertake to mitigate harmful effects of migration, but we need to determine the scope of these restraints and also reflect on what justice requires if people's exercise of their rights harms third parties. With regard to rights, it may be unjust to restrict people's mobility or to compel them to work in certain sectors, but more modest proposals such as taxation or some other form of compensation could be justified. Also, harms incurred through migration may give rise to institutional obligations that a just society must fulfill in ways that may not directly involve emigration. The presence of harmful brain drain might impose obligations in sending countries to build institutions and on receiving countries to facilitate development.

To build an account of how individuals, states, and other actors should address brain drain, it is helpful to survey some of the most prominent proposals. Proposed remedies for harms caused in part by the absence of skilled workers include:

(a) Restrictions on emigration imposed by sending countries
(b) Bonding (for employees who have received public education)
(c) Restrictions on immigration imposed by receiving countries
(d) Compensation for costs paid by migrants
(e) The adoption of ethical recruitment practices
(f) Compensation paid by receiving countries (e.g. fee for costs of training workers, development aid)

I consider each in turn to identify the potential ethical and empirical pitfalls of some approaches to survey promising, morally justifiable strategies for mitigating harmful effects and for promoting the beneficial effects of skilled migration. I consider proposals a–c that involve the restriction of emigration the least promising, whereas proposals d–f suggest reforms that provide elements of an institutional approach to skilled migration.

1.1. Emigration restrictions

The most straightforward response to brain drain is to prevent skilled workers from leaving. Recently, Lea Ypi has proposed that an egalitarian theory of justice in emigration 'requires placing restrictions on emigration when it threatens to reduce the general welfare of citizens in sending societies' (Ypi 2008, p. 411). By emigration restrictions, I understand policies that prevent skilled workers from leaving because they possess skills that are valuable to their community. I consider below the case of bonding which justifies the temporary restriction of emigration in exchange for the state support for education. Though emigration restrictions seem a plausible way of addressing concerns of distributive justice, there are principled and practical reasons for rejecting emigration restrictions and for doubting that this is a very fruitful way of considering the distributive effects of skilled migration.

My strategy in this section is consists in four points. First, I question the moral permissibility of emigration restrictions: there are moral reasons that suggest that it is impermissible under most circumstances to use coercion to prevent people from leaving their country. Second, I draw on the literature on transnationalism to question whether people's obligations neatly map onto population of their national territory. The possibility of transnational special obligations significantly complicates the implications for emigration and for migration more generally. Third, I suggest that if would-be migrants have special obligations to their compatriots, these obligations can usually be met in ways that do not require forgoing migration. Finally, I point to a practical obstacle to implementing just emigration restrictions.

First, emigration restrictions absent compelling justification are generally believed to violate fundamental rights. Emigration restrictions persist in some parts of the world – including de facto restrictions where parts of the population are unable to access exit visas that they are legally entitled to (De Haas and Vezzoli 2011, p. 23) – but these are generally considered morally problematic. The right to emigrate is enshrined in Article 13 of the UN Declaration of Human Rights and Article 12 of the International Covenant on Civil and Political Rights. The International Covenant admits no restriction to emigration 'except those provided by law necessary to protect national security, public order, public health or morals or the rights and freedoms of others' (Bueno de Mesquita and Gordon 2005, p. 15). Any measures that derogate the right to emigration must be 'strictly required by the exigencies of the situation' and subject to the principle of proportionality. Freedom of emigration is a fundamental means of exercising individual self-determination through exit rights (Harvey and Barnidge 2005) as well as a possible condition for realizing one's own conception of the good (Hidalgo 2014).

Do the possibly harmful effects of brain drain meet the threshold necessary for derogating the right to emigrate? To answer this question, we need to ask whether it is just to single out co-nationals possessing scarce, valuable skills for a responsibility to remain, and to contribute through one's profession to the building of institutions. These obligations could arise because migrants have duties to co-nationals that override their right to seek employment outside of their community. Another possibility is that migrants have received state-funded education, which entails an obligation to render services to their national community.

My goal is not to refute all claims that emigration can be restricted, but rather to show that many attempts to restrict emigration are morally problematic and that there are generally better ways of addressing any adverse effects of emigration.[1] Kieran Oberman's recent discussion of when rich states can use brain drain to justify immigration restrictions provides helpful guidance for the question of emigration restrictions. Oberman holds that there must be a strong justification for coercing people. People can be justly coerced only when they have a moral duty to perform the coerced action and when this moral duty can justly be enforced using coercion. Skilled workers can only be coerced if they do in fact have a moral duty to assist their poor compatriots by staying and working and if the state that coerces them is entitled to do so. Since the right to emigrate protects fundamental interests such as the ability to effectively pursue one's conception of the good life, a strong justification must be provided for its abrogation. He summarizes these conditions in terms of three demanding conditions: (1) the skilled worker owes a duty of assistance to poor compatriots, (2) she has a duty to stay in her country to fulfill this duty (as opposed to paying a tax or some other form of compensation), and (3) the state of origin is entitled to enforce this duty (which occurs only if the state has no means of assisting poor members that do not involve migration controls) (Oberman 2013, p. 434).[2] Following Oberman, we can ask whether skilled workers do in fact have obligations toward their compatriots and, if so, whether this obligation needs to be defused by remaining in one's country to work.

Why might would-be emigrants have an obligation to remain to help poor compatriots? Prominent arguments for special obligations hold that people acquire these obligations as part of a system of cooperation, because they jointly subject each other to coercive institutions, or because they share a common identity (Beitz 1979, Miller 1995, Blake 2001, c.f. Blake and Brock forthcoming). These arguments can be extended to emigrants by claiming that skilled workers who desire to emigrate have accumulated debts to their compatriots by participating in systems of cooperation or coercion that oblige them to remain or because their shared identity entails obligations to their formative community.

This brings me to my second point that special obligations may not be contained within national territories. The claim that people have special obligations to compatriots that affect their right to emigrate deserves scrutiny. Even if people have some special obligations to the people living in the same national territory, it might also be the case that they have equally strong obligations to people abroad. Webs of cooperation, shared subjection to coercion, and national identity often span national boundaries. Arguments for emigration restriction often presuppose methodological nationalism with 'nationally bounded societies as the natural unit of analysis' (Wimmer and Glick Schiller 2003, p. 579). Much of the language of brain drain assumes without argument that societies are starkly divided into sending and receiving societies and that individuals belong to only one society and have special duties only to compatriots. This does not capture how people's dual or multiple memberships and loyalties have led to social spaces that inhabit multiple geographical spaces. Revolutions in communication and transportation have contributed to time-space compressions that causally link people in networks. Of particular interest are 'transmigrants' who 'develop and maintain multiple relations – familial, economic, social, organization, religious, and political that span borders' (Glick Schiller et al. 1992, p. 1). Scholars of transnationalism have argued that this assumption often distorts our understanding of the nature of migration flows and their influence on development (Bauböck 1998).

Though there are historical antecedents to transnationalism, capitalist expansion in recent decades has insured that transnational social and economic networks are much more common today. As a consequence, the scope of many people's obligations is unlikely to be limited to their nation-state because the boundaries of their communities diverge from the geographical territory of their state and because transnational causal forces facilitate and compel movement across borders. This has the potential to significantly complicate people's moral obligations with potentially counterintuitive implications. For example, if states can justifiably override people's preferences regarding where they live as advocates of emigration restrictions insist, then foreign skilled workers who have no desire to emigrate may find that special obligations due to cooperation, coercion, or shared identity entail an obligation to immigrate to regions where their skilled are especially valuable.

My third point is that even if we assume that special obligations are largely confined among people within the boundaries of a national territory, it is not clear why the moral obligations of skilled workers can only be defused by remaining within the territory of their community. I discuss below the possibility that migrants could pay a fee or a tax in compensation for benefits received or to diffuse obligations toward poorly off members of their former territory of residence. Here, I want to point out that normative theorists writing on migration often reveal a 'sedentary bias' that assumes migration is abnormal (Dumitru 2009, pp. 37–38). This bias fails to consider the cost to the world of people who choose not to migrate. Indeed, reflection on co-nationals' special obligations might entail that they are required *to emigrate* when emigration is a more effective way of helping compatriots through remittances and other measures. After all, some states encourage emigration of low-skilled workers (e.g. Bangladeshi migrant workers in the Gulf States) and highly skilled workers (e.g. Philippine health care professionals). If we take special obligations seriously, perhaps these states would be justified in forcing some workers to go abroad.

Finally, there is a practical obstacle to proposals to restrict emigration that should give pause to normative theorists who find emigration restrictions attractive. De Haas and Vezzoli argue that though states have considerable influence in structuring emigration patterns, only strong states are able to control emigration and only authoritarian states are willing to do so (De Haas and Vezzoli 2011). The measures needed to prevent people who want to leave from emigrating involve a level of surveillance and coercion of individuals – including the punishment of failed emigrants – that liberal democracies abjure. This poses a dilemma. Policies to restrict emigration that respect people's fundamental rights are unlikely to succeed if people have good reasons for leaving. But if a state decides to implement emigration restrictions on skilled workers that *are* likely to succeed, it would need to adopt unjust policies and this would undermine a legitimate claim to force people to stay.

1.2. Bonding

Another proposal is not to outright prevent highly skilled emigration, but rather to impose some restrictions through monetary or in-kind bonding. Monetary bonding requires that skilled emigrants pay a fee to compensate for the cost of their education; in-kind bonding demands that skilled workers complete a period of service (Cole 2010, p. 122). Usually the ground for bonding is that graduates have benefited from public support for their education. Bonding functions as a temporary restriction on emigration and is often justified on the grounds that people receiving public education have freely entered into an implicit or explicit contract to repay benefits received.

Though bonding has plausibility as a measure to fairly compensate for lost human capital, it too faces moral and practical concerns. First, in the case of in-kind bonding, we might ask how 'voluntary' is it for people to restrict their freedom of occupation and movement for a significant period after studying. The people that have to enter into these sorts of contracts to pursue their education are likely to be among the more vulnerable segments of the educated population. This objection may be overcome in some circumstances, but the conditions of choice must be carefully scrutinized.

Second, if we see bonding as a permissible measure to insure repayment of public services, then the state may have a moral claim to the services of most citizens. Many members of a legitimate, functioning state have received benefits in excess of their contributions. It seems morally arbitrary to compel only those who possess highly valued skills to a period of indentured labor (Cole 2010, p. 125). The fact that people with more natural ability or who possess special skills have chosen certain professions may justify compelling them to contribute more income for redistribution, but taxation for redistribution will not generally centrally affect people's plans and relationships to the degree that the temporary restriction of freedom of movement and occupation would do (Blake and Brock forthcoming).

Bonding also faces practical obstacles if its purpose is to make it more likely that people with skills build institutions that lead to long-term growth. If the purpose of restricting emigration is to build institutions, recently graduated workers are unlikely to contribute to this task because they lack the experience, connections, or the long-term time commitment to accomplish much. Perhaps their labor will enable the state to recoup some of the costs of educating them, but it is unlikely to be an effective remedy to the conditions that encourage skilled workers to leave (Bueno de Mesquita and Gordon 2005, p. 57).

1.3. Immigration restrictions

Another possibility is that receiving states act on behalf of vulnerable developing world countries by refusing to extend visas to skilled workers. Kieran Oberman tells us that 'When a rich state cannot use its own resources to compensate for the effects of deleterious brain drain, then the rich state may indeed be justified in imposing immigration restrictions' (Oberman 2013, p. 447, c.f. Bader 2005, pp. 340–344). Oberman sees restricting immigration as a possible tool for developed states to discharge their obligation to the global poor, though, as we saw above, he only considers its use permissible in cases in which (1) skilled workers have duties to help their poor compatriots, (2) these duties entail that they remain in their country of origin, (3) the country of origin has a right to enforce immigration restriction, and, most importantly for a discussion of immigration restrictions, (4) developed states have in fact discharged their other obligations to aid.

Cases where rich countries have discharged these obligations will be very rare and there are two major practical obstacles. First, developed states mostly use migration policy to attract people with high human capital and to maintain a precarious 'low-skilled' population of exploitable laborers either abroad or in informal markets (Sager 2012a). Real-world policy is precisely the opposite of Oberman's proposal and this is unlikely to change in the near future in today's world of self-interested states. Second, even if some developed states were committed to migration policies that aid the developing world, the states they cannot compensate with resources rather than migration restrictions would likely be ruled by authoritarian regimes. People under these regimes have good reasons to leave and it hardly seems just to prevent them from doing so in the name of justice.

1.4. Bhagwati tax

Instead of directly regulating migration flows by preventing people from leaving, by making education contingent on the acceptation of bonding, or by restricting immigration, it may be possible to mitigate the effects of deleterious skilled migration indirectly by asking them to pay part of their income to benefit people in their country of origin. Jagdish Bhagwati has argued that skilled migrants should pay a tax on their income for a significant period after their emigration (Bhagwati 1979). The tax would ideally be administered at the level of the UN with assistance from developed countries' tax officials. Bhagwati and his colleagues have spent considerable effort in exploring the economics of the proposed tax, as well as its legal ramifications (Bhagwati 1976).

Bhagwati proposes two moral arguments in favor of his tax. The first argument notes that immigration restrictions permit skilled emigrants to extract rents – those lucky enough to receive a visa receive much higher incomes due to artificially restricted competition. It is justifiable, in his view, to tax the windfall gains of those fortunate enough to migrate. The underlying principle of this argument is that *everyone* benefiting from rents caused by the artificial restrictions in the labor market ought to compensate those excluded. Though this principle has considerable plausibility, it is more suited as grounds for greater redistribution at the global level rather than as a reason for taxing the labor of skilled migrants. It hardly seems fair to single out skilled emigrants for taxation – after all, they have benefited from rents less than native born citizens in high wage regions.

Bhagwati presents another argument based on transnational ties: migrants frequently maintain ties across border and in many cases retain voting rights (IDEA 2007). He suggests that these external voting rights amount to 'representation without taxation.' Against the objection that requiring migrants to pay taxes to their countries of origin is unfair, given that they are also taxed in their country of residence, he contends that migrants who want to continue to enjoy the benefits of citizenship in their countries of origin, should pay their fair share. The tax on wages should not be onerous and emigrants can renounce their citizenship if they would prefer to not to pay it (though renunciation will depend in part on receiving citizenship somewhere else in the world). Bhagwati's proposal is a step in the right direction. It seeks to alter institutions (in this case governing taxation) in a way that mitigates harmful effects and more equitably distributes resources.

1.5. Ethical recruiting

Ethical recruiting tries to minimize the possible harmful effects of brain drain by avoiding active recruitment from vulnerable regions and by creating partnerships with source countries in the developing world to mitigate harms and to build capacity (Buchan and Dovlo 2004). Though in many cases recruitment agencies helpfully connect employers and employees, cases where recruiters wield asymmetrical power to trigger and sustain harmful migration flows can be morally problematic. For example, practices of actively recruiting workers from vulnerable regions may violate negative rights to not harm when it foreseeably interferes with states' ability to guarantee the basic rights of its population (Sager 2010). Ethical recruitment changes the focus from potential migrants to practices and institutions. Recruitment may play a part in exacerbating the effects of structural injustice, but we should not overestimate its importance in a just response to the adverse effects of skilled migration. Recruiting is only problematic if it abets the violation of obligations (e.g. by workers attempting to escape an obligation to compensate their state of origin) or if it causes serious harms by undermining states' abilities to protect basic rights. We should view ethical recruitment as part of a broader strategy to create just migration institutions.

1.6. Compensation and/or aid from receiving countries

Another institutional approach worth considering is to specify conditions in which receiving countries have a duty to compensate sending countries from which they receive skilled immigrants. There are three possible rationales for this compensation. First, we might think that the fact that receiving countries benefit from workers who were trained in the sending countries entails a special positive duty to compensate. Second, migration policies might violate negative duties by promoting policies that contribute to undermining the ability of sending states to provide their population with basic entitlements (Sager 2010). Insofar as receiving states knowingly support and benefit from these policies, they may have obligations to mitigate their effects and compensation may be a part of this mitigation.

A third rationale is to assume that irrespective of specific migration patterns, rich states have obligations of international distributive justice that may include compensating regions from which it accepts skilled workers not because they are 'poaching' workers but because aid in these regions will do a great deal of good. For example, the Global Commission on International

Migration (GCIM) states that 'it is essential for foreign aid and investment to be more carefully directed towards countries and sectors that have been particularly affected by the loss of their professionals' (Global Commission on International Migration 2005, p. 25). The report recommends co-investment programs, where developed states provide educational resources to develop professionals who benefit both sending and receiving states. Insofar as these sorts of win-win scenarios are feasible, they should be explored.

The danger of this proposal, however, is that it risks oversimplifying the relationship between compensation and foreign aid and migration. The GCIM's suggestion that foreign aid and investment target areas that have lost skilled professionals may not have the effects envisioned. Migration and development are complements, not substitutes, and development actually increases the flow of people across borders in the short to middle term. Migration tends to follow an inverted U-curve where increased development initially leads to more migration (De Haas 2006). Development leads to rural to urban migration and then often to international migration by providing people with the resources and the knowledge of opportunities in other regions.

Nonetheless, these types of institutional solutions – the taxation of migrants, the restructuring of international recruitment practices, and the strategic use of compensation and aid – help us better envisage how we should approach brain drain. We need to locate skilled migration and migration more generally within the broader 'migration-development nexus' and to provide an account of the institutional conditions under which migration would not contribute to unjust harms. I now turn to this question.

2. An institutional approach to ethics, migration, and development

The focus on brain drain in isolation has distracted attention from more fundamental issues that only become apparent when we move from a consideration of skilled migration to a consideration of migration more generally and when we study it as part of larger economic, social, and political systems. Much of the normative literature on migration has overlooked how migration and development occur in larger structural contexts and thus fails to incorporate morally relevant causal factors into its normative analysis. A full analysis of the morality of migration would include an examination of the effect of security regimes on refugee flows, smuggling and trafficking regimes, and other human rights abuses. Since our topic is on distributive justice, I focus on the 'migration-development nexus.'

First, I discuss the morality of internal migration as a strategy for identifying the conditions under which migration ceases to have morally problematic distributive effects. This reveals the advantages of an institutional approach that goes beyond considerations of the regulation of skilled migration. Second, I argue that global institutions that mediate migration and development are unjust and make some proposals for what is needed so that skilled migration ceases to raise moral qualms.

2.1. The analogy to internal migration

An analogy to domestic migration is useful for clarifying the morality of skilled migration. From the perspective of moral urgency, the focus on *international* brain drain is puzzling. Doctors do not only leave Malawi and South Africa for England and Australia; they also move from rural villages to Lilongwe and to Cape Town. If anything, the effects of internal brain drain are more devastating to the people left behind (Skeldon 2005).

What role, then, does migration play in a theory of justice for a nation-state? If we were to consult major accounts in the philosophical literature on distributive justice in closed societies, we would conclude that migration plays *no* major role in distributive justice. The possibility that the internal distribution of human capital should serve as a fundamental tool for domestic justice is not on the agenda. Theorists of distributive justice do not consider the possibility of using migration policies for redistributive purposes.

Is this an oversight or an appropriate policy response to 'internal brain drain'? In the United States, not only rural areas but urban centers such as Las Vegas and Detroit suffer from health care shortages (Association of American Medical Colleges 2012). What should the government do to insure that all Americans have access to adequate medical services? More generally, what policies should be pursued for impoverished areas to mitigate the effects of out-migration? Should the United States mirror policy advice on brain drain by preventing or mitigating the movement of skilled labor, perhaps by in-kind bonding of Nevada-trained doctors and Michigan-trained engineers or by setting up internal border controls?

This would be a mistake. If it turns out that economic decline is due to bad local policies, then the best solution is to reform laws and policies and to build infrastructure, rather than target individual workers. Policy-makers should do their best to promote the well-being of their constituents. But this is not easily done – building institutions is difficult in any circumstances and their success depends on many factors outside of the control of policy-makers. In some cases, it may not be possible. Lant Pritchett notes that technological and economic shifts can lead to region-specific shocks, where the optimal population declines (Pritchett 2006). Even if these regions had good institutions and policies, their economies do not sustain as many people as before. A historical example is the ghost towns of the North American gold rush. A contemporary example is the US rust belt. Pritchett dubs regions where the optimal population has declined as ghosts or as zombies. In ghost regions, the population has left; in zombie regions, the population is unable to leave and the consequence is high unemployment and low wages. During structural economic changes, some people will undoubtedly suffer. We should do what we can to ease this suffering, but it cannot be entirely avoided. When the attempt to retain skilled workers fails, one of the major options for people with limited opportunities is to leave.

This suggests that the neglect of skilled internal migration is not an oversight in the literature on distributive justice; it reflects a better approach to addressing possible harmful effects of migration. Few people in well-functioning states complain that students pay reduced in-state tuition rates and then move to another region after graduation or suggest that students in key professions are morally required to commit to a period of service in return for their subsidized education. Programs such as the US Public Service Loan Forgiveness are based not on the moral obligation of students to repay society, but rather as compensation for supererogatory service (e.g. in the military) or as a mechanism to enable people to perform public service without being overwhelmed by crushing student debt. The lack of a movement to curb the internal movement of graduating students is not just because most people accept that the right to movement within one's state is fundamental. Rather, just background institutions mitigate concerns that internal migrants unjustly cause hardship. Freedom of movement within one's state is one of those institutions that protect people from internal brain drain. For similar reasons, skilled migration between developed countries is usually seen as 'brain exchange' and is not considered a problem of justice. Rather than being a 'drain' on sending countries, skilled migration between developed countries efficiently allocates human capital between regions whose residents enjoy good institutions.

Can we imagine a scenario in which internal migration would be morally problematic? Migration would only become problematic under situations in which government policies undermined institutions in some regions by unfairly allocating resources or by enforcing laws that discriminate against some regionally concentrated groups. Out-migration might exacerbate the effects of bad or unjust institutions. But in this case, it is not migration itself that is morally problematic, but rather the bad government policies that cause people to leave. The badness of brain drain derives from unjust institutional structures under which migration causes harm.

2.2. Institutional harms and international migration

In the domestic case, skilled migration only indirectly raises issues of justice. The situation of international migration is similar. Skilled migration is one factor that an account of global justice must address, but it is rarely a fundamental cause of failed institutions. Nonetheless, current global institutions are structured by power asymmetries which have led to migration policies that, together with other policies affecting developing countries, systematically harm poor and vulnerable people. Brain drain needs to be understood in this context since the focus on skilled migration mistakes an indicator of deeper structural problems (i.e. people leaving) for the structural problems themselves. Our focus should be on structural changes that spur migration and on the role of migration in sustaining and exacerbating their harmful effects.

We should combine an ethical perspective that attributes moral responsibility to agents who unjustly harm others or who uphold institutions that are known to cause unjust harms and an empirical framework that acknowledges the role of global institutions in shaping migration flows. Neither the ethical perspective nor the empirical framework is meant to be comprehensive. There are other moral aspects of migration policy (including the obligation to fulfill more general duties of humanity and to respect basic liberties). My account rests on this minimalistic account of global institutional justice and the plausibility that the 'migration-development nexus' includes institutions that are indeed unjust.

The moral account holds that people who play a causal role in upholding unjust institutions and structures are partly morally responsible for these institutions (Pogge 2002). In the case of international migration, we need to address the moral responsibility for global and transnational institutions and structures. I propose a modest distributive principle: global institutions should not systematically disadvantage people so that they are unable to access adequate resources and freedoms. The global basic structure does not need to optimize human well-being (or capabilities), but it should not actively promote asymmetrical distributions. For example, if people interfere with domestic institution building (e.g. through aggressive recruitment or unfair trade practices) or cause misery by transforming developing economies, they acquire moral responsibilities for those harmed.

Do the institutions structuring migration indeed inflict harms? The normative literature on brain drain has often explicitly or implicitly assumed models of migration that ignore structural factors (Sager 2012b). Migration is seen from a neo-classical economic standpoint where people from low-wage regions relocate to areas in which they can receive a higher return on their human capital (Borjas 1989). The decision to migrate is treated as an individual cost–benefit analysis. Moral analysis aggregates the effects of individual decisions and balances the costs and benefits to people from sending regions against the cost and benefits to migrants and people in receiving regions. The debate becomes a matter of determining the effects of lost human capital, remittances, skill transfer, and other factors.

Neo-classical models of migration capture the important insight that wage differentials play an important role in decisions to migrate, but their failure to address structural factors leaves them incapable of explaining particular migration flows. The focus on individuals distracts attention from the factors that motivate people to leave and the interactions between migration, capital flows, norms, and government policies. Instead of asking whether it is just to prevent skilled workers from migrating, we need to examine the conditions that make migration a preferred decision and to ask if the causes that generate and sustain these conditions are just.

The analysis of internal migration in countries with well-functioning institutions alerts us to how local and national institutional failures are often the source of injustice. Though a comprehensive account of justice in migration would address local and national institutions in detail, my focus is on how national institutions are partly upheld by a global order. We must study the causes of migration together with the consequences of migration as the relationship between migration and development is reciprocal (De Haas 2008). Migrants respond to local development contexts that determine their quality of life, affect their aspirations to migrate, and promote their capability to do so. The local development context is partly determined by the macro (national, international) development context which also shapes migrants' aspirations and opportunities to migrate. Once people begin to migrate, they may transform the local development context which in turn reshapes people's aspirations (e.g. through the creation of migration networks). Over the long run, migration may affect the macro development context, especially if migrants establish technology bridges and transfer skills.

At an international level, developed states dictate migration policy to the rest of the world, often through international institutions; the global South has far less power to influence policies and principles (Sørensen 2012, p. 62). This occurs within the context of global capitalism, where major actors such as multinational corporations have lobbied for policies at the international level and within developed states to open capital and labor markets (Skeldon 1997, p. 25). Neo-liberal economic globalization has structurally transformed societies to create flexible and precarious labor markets and to dismantle welfare states (Delgado Wise and Márquez Covarrubias 2010). In much of the developing world, rural to urban migration is partly a result of economic shocks in which technological and structural changes lower the optimal population of rural regions. This has occurred through practices such as land enclosures, the extraction of natural resources, export processing zones, and military interventions imposed from or influenced by outside powers (Massey *et al.* 1998).

We should avoid simplistic views that treat developing countries as passive and exploitable victims, ignore potential benefits, and deny people in the developing world agency (De Haas 2008). Nonetheless, the insight remains that capitalist expansion has structured migration networks so that developing countries and their migrants have mostly had to adapt to imposed conditions rather than to negotiate fair terms. Saskia Sassen's research on the global city reveals both transnational markets between global cities for highly skilled professions and 'circuits of survival' following transnational 'care chains' partly generated by onerous economic policies imposed on the Global South (Sassen 2008). Transnational migration systems structure these migration flows into bifurcated labor markets sustained through transnational economic and social structures. In some cases, the exodus of skilled workers, particularly from small countries with relatively little educational infrastructure, exacerbates wider development problems. When this occurs, there is an obligation to structure global institutions so they do not predictably harm the worst off members of the human population by making it unlikely that the people best placed to help are most likely to leave. Since migration and development policies influence each other, the goal is to promote positive feedback loops.

In sum, we should seek a world in which the migration of skilled workers benefits or at least does not harm vulnerable people. This mostly involves the guarantee of just institutions since questions of institutional justice and in many cases institutional reform will only indirectly involve migration. Nonetheless, one reason that people are vulnerable to economic shifts and the flight of talent is the lack of mobility. Global policies in which developed states shape migration flows to recruit talent while excluding low-skilled workers or to forcing them into shadow market or exploitative guest worker programs exacerbate harms. If we are indeed concerned about brain drain and not merely using it as an excuse to maintain exclusionary migration practices or to shirk duties of global distributive justice, we need to examine migration as a whole as well as to explore its interaction with development policies.

The most promising migration policies that might ameliorate brain drain over the long run would involve lifting the prerogative of sovereign states to shape migration policy in their perceived self-interest and to improve market distorting policies and practices such as temporary worker programs or the reliance on unauthorized labor. These policies lower the wages of migrants, reduce remittances, and, in the case of restrictive border controls, reduce circular migration. Migration can be part of a general development strategy, but only if accompanied with broader national and local institutional reform that encourage investment and return migration. Insofar as global institutions hinder the development of just national and local institutions, there is a moral duty to transform them. Skilled migration flows will not pose problems of distributive justice if they take place against relative justice background institutions.

3. Conclusion

Normative theorists of immigration are rightly concerned about how migration distributes benefits and burdens. To answer this question, it is necessary to understand how migration interacts with other policies to encourage or hinder development. It is impossible to determine the distributive effects of migration without taking into account the many structures and causes of international movement, the work experiences of those who move, the transfer of remittances and skills, and the ability of states and other agents to provide services. I have tried to show that an adequate moral response to skilled migration should not be concerned with emigrants in isolation, but should rather focus on how institutions sometimes lead to skilled migration having deleterious effects. When we reframe the brain drain, it becomes evident that skilled migration in isolation should not be the focus for an account justice in migration. Rather, we need a holistic assessment of the economic and social background institutions against which migration occurs. Moral responsibility for possible harms to people left behind does not rest primarily on people who wish to leave their countries of origin, irrespective of their education or skills. Instead, justice requires reshaping institutions so that migration does not adversely affect the people left behind, and, more ambitiously, so that it fairly distributes benefits across borders.

Acknowledgments

I would like to thank Crispino Akakpo, Patti Lenard, and an anonymous referee for their comments on this manuscript.

Notes

1. For a sophisticated discussion of the limitations of arguments from cooperation, coercion, and shared identity to restrict emigration, see Michael Blake's chapters in his forthcoming book on brain drain co-authored with Gillian Brock (Blake and Brock forthcoming).
2. Oberman (2013, p. 434) states a fourth condition that rich states have 'the legitimacy to impose counter-brain-drain immigration restrictions.'

References

Association of American Medical Colleges. 2012. *Recent studies and reports on physician shortages in the US*. Center for Workforce Studies. Available from: https://www.aamc.org/download/100598/data/recentworkforcestudies.pdf.

Bach, S., 2008. International mobility of health professionals: brain drain or brain exchange? *In*: A. Solimano, ed. *The international mobility of talent: types, causes, and development impact*. New York: Oxford University Press, 202–235.

Bader, V., 2005. The ethics of immigration. *Constellations*, 12, 331–361.

Bauböck, R., 1998. The crossing and blurring of boundaries in international migration. challenges for social and political theory. *In*: R. Bauböck and J. Rundell, eds. *Blurred boundaries: migration, ethnicity, citizenship*. Aldershot: Ashgate, 17–52.

Beitz, C.R., 1979. *Political theory and international relations*. Princeton, NJ: Princeton University Press.

Bhagwati, J.N., ed., 1976. *Taxing the brain drain, vol. 1: a proposal*. Amsterdam: North-Holland.

Bhagwati, J.N., 1979. International migration of the highly skilled: economics, ethics and taxes. *Third world quarterly*, 1, 17–30.

Blake, M., 2001. Distributive justice, state coercion, and autonomy. *Philosophy and public affairs*, 30, 257–296.

Blake, M. and Brock, G., forthcoming. *The ethics of emigration: debating brain drain*. New York: Oxford University Press.

Borjas, G., 1989. Economic theory and international migration. *International migration review*, 23 (3), 457–485.

Buchan, J. and Dovlo, D., 2004. *International recruitment of health workers to the UK: a report for DFID*. London: DFID Health Systems Resource Center.

Bueno de Mesquita, J. and Gordon, M., 2005. *The international migration of health workers: a human rights analysis*. London: Medact.

Carens, J., 1992. Migration and morality: a liberal egalitarian perspective. *In*: B. Barry and R.E. Goodin, eds. *Free movement: ethical issues in the transnational migration of people and money*. University Park: Pennsylvania State University Press, 25–47.

Clemens, M., 2007. *Do visas kill? Health effects of African health professional emigration*. Washington, DC: Center for Global Development.

Cole, P.A., 2010. The right to leave versus a duty to remain. *In*: R. Shah, ed. *Global health, justice, and the brain drain*. Basingstoke: Palgrave-McMillan, 118–129.

De Haas, H., 2006. *Turning the tide? Why 'development instead of migration' policies are bound to fail*. Oxford: International Migration Institute, University of Oxford.

De Haas, H., 2008. *Migration and development: a theoretical perspective*. International Migration Institute.

De Haas, H. and Vezzoli, S., 2011. *Leaving matters: the nature, evolution and effects of emigration policies*. Oxford: IMI Working Papers Series.

Delgado Wise, R. and Márquez Covarrubias, H., 2010. Understanding the relationship between migration and development: toward a new theoretical approach. *In*: N.G. Schiller and T. Faist, eds. *Migration, development and transnationalization: a critical stance*. New York: Berghahn Books, 142–175.

Docquier, F. and Abdelslam, M., 2006. *Brain drain and inequality among nations*. Bonn: Institute for the Study of Labor. Available from: http://ftp.iza.org/dp2440.pdf.

Dumitru, S., 2009. Emigración, Talentos y Justicia: Un Argumento Feminista sobre la Fuga de Cerebros [Emigration, talents, and justice: a feminist argument on the brain drain]. *Isonomía*, 30, 32–52.

Glick Schiller, N., Basch, L. and Blanc-Szanton, C., 1992. *Towards a transnational perspective on migration*. New York: The New York Academy of Sciences.

Global Commission on International Migration. 2005. *Migration in an interconnected world: new directions for action*. Versoix: SRO-Kundig. Available from: http://www.queensu.ca/samp/migrationresources/reports/gcim-complete-report-2005.pdf

Harvey, C. and Barnidge, Jr., R.P., 2005. *The right to leave one's own country under international law*. Global Commission on International Migration (GCIM). Available from: http://www.peacepalacelibrary.nl/ebooks/files/GCIM_TP8.pdf

Hidalgo, J.S., 2014. Freedom, immigration, and adequate options. *Critical review of international social and political philosophy*, 17, 189–221.

International Institute for Democracy and Electoral Assistance (IDEA) and Instituto Federal Electoral de Mexico (IFE). 2007. *Voting from abroad. The international IDEA handbook*. Stockholm and Mexico City: IDEA and IFE.

Kapur, D. and McHale, M., 2005. *Give us your best and brightest*. Washington, DC: Center for Global Development.

Massey, D.G., *et al.*, 1998. *Worlds in motion*. New York: Clarendon Press.

Miller, D., 1995. *On Nationality*. Oxford: Clarendon Press.

Mills, E.J., *et al.*, 2011. The financial cost of doctors emigrating from sub-Saharan Africa: human capital analysis. *British medical journal*, 343. Available from: http://www.bmj.com/content/343/bmj.d7031.

Mullan, F., 2005. The metrics of the physician brain drain. *New England journal of medicine*, 353, 1810–1818.

Oberman, K., 2013. Can brain drain justify immigration restrictions? *Ethics*, 123, 427–455.

Pogge, T., 2002. *World poverty and human rights*. Cambridge: Polity Press.

Pritchett, L., 2006. *Let their people come*. Washington, DC: Center for Global Development.

Sager, A., 2010. Brain drain, health, and global justice. *In*: R. Shah, ed. *The international migration of health workers: ethics, rights, and justice*. New York: Palgrave-McMillan, 103–117.

Sager, A., 2012a. Immigration, class, and global justice: some moral considerations/ implications. *In*: M. Labelle, J. Couture and R. Frank, eds. *La communauté politique en question*. Montreal: UQAM Press, 29–46.

Sager, A., 2012b. The implications of migration theory for distributive justice. *Global justice: theory, practice, and rhetoric*, 5, 56–70.

Sahay, A., 2009. *Indian diaspora in the United States: brain drain or gain?* New York: Rowman & Littlefield Publishers.

Sassen, S., 2008. Two stops in today's new global geographies: shaping novel labor supplies and employment regimes. *American behavioral scientist*, 52, 457–496.

Skeldon, R., 2005. Globalisation, skilled migration and poverty alleviation: brain drains in context. Brighton: Development Research Centre on Migration, Globalisation & Poverty, University of Sussex. Available from: http://www.migrationdrc.org/ publications/working_papers/WP-T15.pdf

Sørensen, N.N., 2012. Revisiting the migration-development nexus: from social networks and remittances to markets for migration control. *International migration*, 50 (3), 61–76.

Tesón, F.R., 2008. Brain drain. *San Diego law review*, 45, 899–932.

Van Eyck, K., 2004. *Women and international migration in the health sector*. Geneva: Public Services International.

Wimmer, A. and Glick Schiller, N., 2003. Methodological nationalism, the social sciences, and the study of migration: an essay in historical epistemology. *International migration review*, 37 (3), 576–610.

Ypi, L., 2008. Justice in migration: a closed borders utopia? *The journal of political philosophy*, 16, 391–418.

Temporary migration projects and voting rights

Valeria Ottonelli[a] and Tiziana Torresi[b]

[a]Philosophy Department, Università di Genova, Genova, Italy; [b]School of History and Politics, University of Adelaide, Adelaide, Australia

Theorists have recently argued that in order to protect migrants from vulnerability and domination, host countries should grant voting rights to all residents, including those who are present on the territory on a temporary visa. Although we endorse the inclusive and egalitarian rationale of this approach, we argue that it is based on the presumption that all migrants aim at permanent inclusion and is therefore inadequate in the case of those who are engaged in 'temporary migration projects'. We suggest that in order to provide these migrants with a form of political voice that fits their life plans, we need to look at different institutional tools than conventional voting rights, and we point to trade unions and migrant organizations as promising alternatives. We also show that, contrary to what may be thought of other forms of temporary mobility, temporary migration projects and the institutional solutions we propose in order to address the needs of the migrants involved are not disruptive of liberal-democratic institutions.

Whether they endorse open borders or a more restrictive immigration policy, most liberal theorists argue that once migrants are allowed into a country they should not be kept indefinitely in a condition of second-class citizenship, but should reasonably soon be granted all the rights that the full members of the society enjoy.

This inclusive stance calls for the extension to migrants not only of civil and social rights, but also of full political rights, including voting rights in national elections. This is required not only to protect them from violence and abuse, but also to avoid forms of social inequality and exclusion that are necessarily disruptive of the liberal-democratic order. The existence of a class of people who are subject to the laws of the country but do not have political voice is the distinctive mark of political domination and a straightforward negation of the democratic principle. In order to make the acquisition of full political rights smoother for migrants, some theorists have advocated a de-nationalized form of citizenship (Kostakopoulou 2008), while others have argued that full political rights should be granted to all migrants, including those who are on a temporary visa (Sager 2014).

We fully endorse the rationale of this inclusive approach, both for those migrants who move on a permanent basis, and for those who suffer the temporariness of their status as a second-best choice due to the constraints imposed by the receiving state. However, we argue that for many others it may be a gravely inadequate response. In fact, contrary to what much normative political theory seems to assume, becoming a permanent member of the receiving society is not the first choice for all migrants. Increasing numbers of migrants do not move to a foreign country with the intention to remain there permanently, or to integrate within the host society, even when they have the opportunity to do so; they plan instead to spend abroad a limited span of time, with the purpose of collecting resources to be invested in their country of origin (Dustmann and Weiss 2007, OECD 2008, Hugo 2009). We call these migratory patterns 'temporary migration projects'.

We argued elsewhere (Ottonelli and Torresi 2012) that putting these migrants on the path to citizenship does not necessarily serve their purposes and life plans and does not remedy the condition of vulnerability that they are likely to suffer in the host society. We argue here that this holds also, and even more obviously, for the proposal to extend to migrants voting rights in the national elections of the host country.

The paper is organized as follows. In section 1, we discuss temporary migration projects and their implications for the condition of the migrants involved in the host society. We argue that because of the marginal and segregated position in which they place themselves, these migrants are highly vulnerable and need to be granted special rights, since conventional citizenship rights will not suffice to protect them. In section 2, we explain why the argument for extending full voting rights to migrants, although very powerful in the case of other categories of foreigners, in this case misses the point of democratic rights, at the instrumental, procedural and symbolic level. In section 3, we suggest that in order to provide these migrants with effective political voice we need to look at different institutional tools than conventional voting rights, and we point to trade unions and migrant labour organizations as promising alternatives. In the final section we argue that, contrary to what may be thought of other forms of temporary mobility, temporary migration projects and the institutional solutions we propose in order to address the needs of the migrants involved are not disruptive of liberal-democratic institutions.

Temporary migration projects

By temporary migration projects we understand the plan to migrate to another country with the intention of spending there a limited, albeit not necessarily brief, amount of time or a series of cyclical, relatively short stays. This time abroad aims to procuring the means to advance specific goals back home (furthering children's education, building a house, supporting a family, starting a new business activity, etc.), often as part of a common project agreed upon by the whole family (Stark 1991, Bauer and Gang 1998). What is distinctive about these migration plans is that the eventual return to the country of origin is not a second-best strategy dictated by the lack of opportunities for permanent moves, nor the result of failed permanent migration. Rather, it results from the social, familial and economic stakes migrants have in their country of origin; given those stakes, migration is not sought as the search for a 'better place to live', but as a way to improve one's status and welfare back home.

This type of migration is best exemplified by the temporary or circular movements within Europe from new EU member countries (European Commission 2009, Black *et al.* 2010, Anghel 2013, Fihel and Grabowska-Lusinska 2014); after the lifting of the legal barriers to free circulation and employment to which they were once subjected, these migrants can now opt for permanent forms of movement; however, many of them engage instead in migratory projects oriented to return and plan their whole migratory experience accordingly. Arguably, even in those contexts in which migrants are subjected to social and legal constraints that would make their choice to move on a permanent basis unfeasible or arduous, we still cannot assume that return is always a second-best choice for migrants. There is growing evidence, indeed, that temporary and circular migration, which is a spreading trend, responds to the interests and plans of many categories of migrants (Dustmann and Weiss 2007, Tsuda 2013).[1]

Of course, the phenomenology of these migratory experiences reflects the specific characteristics of particular migrants, such as their gender, age and cultural origin, as well as the social, economic and cultural contexts in which they take place. However, the specific rationale of these migratory experiences makes it possible to delineate an ideal-typical sketch of the migrants who engage in them.

Migrants engaged in temporary migration projects tend to be older and more skilled than migrants settling permanently (Catania *et al.* 2007, Vadean and Piracha 2009). In some cases, they are more common among members of relatively richer households (Piracha and Vadean 2009). Return migrants are more likely to have children at the time of their first migration, but are less likely to migrate with them than permanent migrants. In this group, spouses, and relatives in general, also remain in the home country (Parreñas 2001, Castagnone *et al.* 2007, Leogrande 2008, Vadean and Piracha 2009).

These migratory strategies are based upon a sharp distinction between the social, civil and political spaces of the sending country, where the life of the migrant is still largely centred, and the destination country (Ottonelli and Torresi 2012). Anthropological studies have found that photographs exchanged by migrants and family members, for example, while serving the purpose of maintaining the connection between the migrant and her family, are also a way of representing and performing this particular type of migration. It becomes the migrant's duty to indicate, in their communication with their family, their continued interest in the life in their home country and to portray the period abroad as an 'empty limbo in which ... life is not lived' (Fedyuk 2012, p. 287).

As a consequence of their projects these migrants behave in distinctive ways in the host society. First, in relation to the labour market, migrants oriented to return are significantly more likely to work while abroad compared to permanent migrants (Vadean and Piracha 2009). They also tend to work longer hours than they would back home, as well as more than non-migrants (Dustmann 1996, Aleman-Castilla 2007). They tend to save more and remit more when compared to permanent migrants (Stark 1991, Bauer and Gang 1998, Collier, Piracha, and Randazzo 2011). Moreover, unlike permanent migrants, there is, for these migrants, an increase in remittance flows as the duration of the period abroad increases (Collier, Piracha, and Randazzo 2011). When investing in human capital, their choice may reflect the specificity of the home country's labour market rather than the host country's one (Dustmann 1996). Finally, these migrants tend to accept lower paid jobs than permanent migrants (Dustmann 1996, Leogrande 2008), as well as jobs with difficult and harsh working conditions (Alexandru 2007, Uccellini 2010). Their earnings tend to be lower than both those of nationals' and permanent migrants'. Some studies also indicate that return migrants are considerably more likely to work illegally than permanent migrants (Vadean and Piracha 2009).

Second, to maximize savings, migrants tend to choose cheap accommodation, often sharing with others considerably sub-standard dwellings (Leogrande 2008). Moreover, accommodation is often impersonal, shows no investment, and looks 'temporary' with few, or no personal items on display, with, sometimes, the exception of small 'shrines' composed of objects from the home country, family pictures, icons, often a national flag (Fedyuk 2012).

Third, migrants engaged in temporary migration projects show limited engagement with the host society at the level of social, civic and political participation. They invest little in the creation of a new life in the host country at the social level. In some cases they acquire only a very basic knowledge of the local language (Castagnone et al. 2007). They display low levels of political engagement and do not actively attempt to better their economic and social conditions in the host country (Hammar 1990, Glystos 1997, Fouron 2003, Stoll and Wong 2007).

These migratory experiences, although legitimate and sensible,[2] expose the migrants to very serious risks and entail a high degree of *vulnerability*. Vulnerability has been variously understood, but is mostly considered to include both internal and external elements, that is to say, characteristics that are inherent to the vulnerable individual or population and characteristics that relate instead to their particular position and circumstances especially in relation to the institutional framework that applies to them (Schroeder and Gefenas 2009).

Migrants engaged in temporary migration projects are vulnerable in two specific ways. First, temporary migration projects are often at high risk of failure for reasons endogenous to the migration project (relationships break down, target savings are not achieved, etc.) but also due to lack of institutional support for these unorthodox life plans. Even when return eventually happens successfully, evidence shows that migrants consistently underestimate the amount of time they will spend in the country of destination (van den Berg and Weynandt 2012). The failure of a temporary migration project, moreover, may result in migrants being left in a sort of limbo where return becomes difficult due to unforeseen circumstances (Castagnone *et al.* 2007) but successful integration within the host society is also very difficult. The migrants, therefore, find themselves trapped and lacking effective *exit options* (Ottonelli and Torresi 2013).

Second, in pursuing their projects, migrants place themselves in a condition of marginality and lesser status in the receiving country. This is psychologically and socially possible for the migrants to accept because of the temporary nature of their migration projects and the sharp distinction between the social spaces of home and destination country. This condition is also in line with the migrants' commitment to saving their earnings and off-work time for when they will return home, but it must inevitably result in a high degree of vulnerability in the receiving society.

It is this specific combination of partially self-imposed marginality and vulnerability that raises important normative questions for liberal political theory. On the one hand, the migrants' chosen lack of civic, social and political investment in the host society makes the traditional 'solution' to the issue of migrants' integration – i.e. their full inclusion through admission to citizenship – unsuitable for these specific migrants. This is for two main reasons. First, because citizenship, in so far as it aims at the creation of a social space of equal membership within the receiving society, is neither desirable nor appropriate for these migrants. Of course, specific benefits and rights attached to citizenship – such as the right to travel freely from and to one's original country – may prove very helpful in carrying out a temporary migration project, and the condition of citizenship is anyway preferable to the harsh conditions often imposed by temporary visas or guest-worker programs; however, the assumptions of stable membership and residence embodied in the conventional social and welfare protections provided by citizenship rights often make them unsuitable to the plans of those engaged in temporary migration projects.[3] Second, the protective role that citizenship rights are meant to perform is based on a number of sociological assumptions about engagement with, and embeddedness in, the society, which make it possible to effectively claim one's rights. These assumptions however, simply do not hold for this category of migrants.

These migrants' condition of vulnerability makes it necessary for the host society, out of fairness to the migrants and concern for the integrity of the society's liberal democratic ethos, to devise an institutional remedy to such condition. To this end, we have argued elsewhere that migrants engaged in temporary migration projects should be granted a set of special rights devised to respond to and recognize their specific life plan, aims and needs, and therefore remedy their specific vulnerabilities, but also signal their special status as temporary 'members' of the community (Ottonelli and Torresi 2012).

The case for granting voting rights to temporary migrants

Putting those engaged in a temporary migration project on the path to full national citizenship and granting them the conventional rights attached to such status is not the right solution to their condition of vulnerability and does not respond to their life plans and goals. However, a legitimate concern might arise that by downplaying the meaning and role of citizenship rights for these migrants we are also giving up too light-heartedly an important set of guarantees usually attached to national citizenship: citizenship comes with political rights, including voting rights at the national level.

Political rights are conventionally seen as an essential guarantee against abuses and exploitation. In this specific case, it could be argued that no civil and social rights, however special and ad hoc, could ever be functional to the life projects of temporary migrants and effective in protecting them in their dealings with the host society unless they are negotiated through, and guaranteed by, a voice by the migrants themselves; and this requires giving them full political rights in the host country.

The case for endowing temporary migrants with voting rights in the national elections of the host country is strengthened by two important considerations, which appear to be in line with our general argument. The first consideration is that, although voting rights are conventionally seen as the mark of full citizenship, they can be conceptually and legally disentangled from it. Citizenship requires a thicker relationship to the host society, and comes with duties and rights (e.g. the right to assistance from one's embassy while abroad or the right to apply for certain jobs or positions) that are not necessarily attached to political rights (Lenard 2012, Sager 2014). Our claim that full citizenship does not fit the plans of the migrants engaged in temporary migration projects, therefore, does not rule out that they should be granted voting rights in the host country.

The second consideration that strengthens the case for granting voting rights to temporary migrants is in line with our analysis of these migrants' vulnerability and the deep relational injustice it brings about within the host society. Focusing on vulnerability, in fact, highlights an especially urgent and widely recognized ground for political rights: having a political voice and being given a share in the exercise of political power is the most prominent antidote against exploitation, domination and abuse. This is true in two senses, one more instrumental, and the other more definitional or procedural. On the instrumentalist side, it might be argued that political rights are the most effective means for defending oneself against abuses and maltreatment. Political rights, therefore, become especially salient when people are highly vulnerable, like in this case. On the procedural side, it may be argued that equality of political voice is a definitional condition of just and equal relations between the people who live in the same society, and conversely the lack of such voice is constitutive of the asymmetrical relations that define and cause migrants' vulnerability. Sager (2014) has aptly conveyed this important claim by appealing to a principle of non-domination. Focusing on domination serves to explain why temporary migrants are entitled to voting rights even if they may not have any long-lasting interests or stakes in the ruling of the host country, which is a condition often assumed as the proper ground for full political rights.[4] Even those migrants who are planning to return home and therefore will not be stable members of the *demos* are subject to the local laws for an extended period of time, including laws that regulate the modalities by which their migration projects can be pursued. Therefore, if not guaranteed by the right to participate in the law-making, they will be exposed to the arbitrary power of the rule-makers, which will substantiate itself in a lower and often degrading status within the host society for those so disenfranchised.

This case for the political voice of temporary migrants seems compelling. However, we argue that the emphasis on voting rights in national elections as a remedy to the vulnerability of all migrants, including those who engage in a temporary migration project, is misguided. This is not because we assume a thick notion of citizenship as a necessary requirement for the enjoyment of voting rights. We grant that the *entitlement* to full voting rights may be separated from a thick conception of citizenship based on national identity and embeddedness in deep and pervasive social relations; moreover, we acknowledge that the specific vulnerability of those engaged in temporary migration projects exposes them to serious forms of domination from the very first moment of their arrival in the host country.[5] However, our claim is that if we want to account for the *meaning* and *effectiveness* of voting rights, we cannot separate them from those aspects of citizenship that serve as preconditions for their effective exercise, and such aspects do in fact presuppose social and material conditions that are lacking in the case of those migrants who are engaged in temporary migration projects.

Voting rights at the national level are no exception to our general treatment of citizenship rights and of the reasons why they are ineffective in the case of these migrants. Indeed, they are the most obvious example of the dangers of what elsewhere we called 'fetishism of rights' (Ottonelli and Torresi 2012): the danger of not realizing that liberal and democratic rights are valuable not just per se, but for the kind of social relations they engender and support, and for the actual protection they provide to the freedom and status of their holders. Political rights lose most of their value when the conditions for what Rawls calls the 'fair value of political liberties' (Rawls 1993) are lacking. And this is exactly the case with migrants engaged in temporary migration projects. Given their specific life plans and migratory projects, these migrants tend to engage at a very superficial level with the host society, and to accept or seek isolation and segregation; they tend to acquire limited knowledge of the local language, are deprived of extended webs of connections and acquaintances, and are unlikely to invest time or resources in the political system of the host country; all this undermines the bases for their effective engagement in the electoral processes and makes their chances of effectively using voting rights at the national level in the host society very low.

To these considerations, which to a certain degree also hold for other social and civil rights, we should add another important point, which is specific to voting rights. In order for temporary migrants' vote to have a weight within existing political systems, it must be appealing to political parties or what we might call in general terms 'electoral entrepreneurs'. These must have some incentive for making political proposals that can gain the vote of those migrants who are planning to return home and some incentives to at least try to be accountable to them. But given the temporary character of their migration project, these potential electors constitute a temporary, unstable and marginal flux of votes whose electoral value would be very low.

It might be objected that these are in fact contingent, consequentialist considerations that do not capture the principled and procedural side of the argument from domination; the ground for giving temporary migrants the right to vote in national elections does not lie only in the expected consequences in terms of what migrants could get from them, but in the simple fact that migrants are subject to the laws of the host country and therefore, if they are not given voting rights, they will be vulnerable to domination, since they will be exposed to the arbitrary will of the citizens. Furthermore, focusing exclusively on consequentialist considerations seems to neglect the symbolic value of voting rights, which express the equal status of all those who live in the same social space and are subject to the same laws (Sager 2014).

It might also be noted that we would abhor resorting to this kind of considerations in the case of other disadvantaged social groups. Arguably, in some societies women, or other marginalised groups, lack the social and material conditions for taking advantage of their political rights, and the value of their vote in the political market is not as high as that of other social groups. They may also be politically unskilled and unorganized, and lack the education – or even the linguistic abilities – to exercise their political rights with full competence. However, we would find it perverse to see these as reasons for disenfranchising them or for discounting the importance of their right to vote in national elections. Why should these arguments not be equally outrageous when applied to migrants engaged in temporary migration projects?

Let us address this last question first, and then respond to the more general criticisms against the apparent consequentialist bias in our argument. There is an important difference between migrants who engage in a temporary migration project and other social groups that are subject to the laws of the host country. As far as the latter are concerned, the lack of the social and cultural preconditions for the full exercise of their political rights should be seen as transitory and unwelcome. Women or members of a disadvantaged minority, at a certain point of the history of a country, may enjoy a lower level of education, social integration or power than other groups; however, citizenship rights are in place exactly in order to remedy as soon as possible these unfavourable circumstances.

The same also holds for those migrants who are kept in a segregated condition by legal provisions and social arrangements that deprive them of fundamental civil rights, make their permanence in the receiving society forcefully temporary by law, or subject them to the always pending threat of deportation or loss of legal status, as it is often the case with current temporary migration programs (Carens 2008). The lack of the conditions for the full political participation of these migrants is imposed on them by unfair arrangements. Also in this case voting rights, although maybe ineffective in the short run, can be defended as a first step towards a path of inclusion and full recognition within the host society.

The case of migrants who make returning home the central goal of their migratory project, however, is very different. Their lack of preconditions for the full exercise of their political liberties is not simply an unwelcome circumstance that burdens their lives, but it is integral to the strategy they adopt for carrying out their life plans. The social integration, engagement with the local political system, and investment in education that their full participation would require would divert energies and resources from their project and purpose, which is to collect capitals in the host country to be spent at home. Of course their social conditions and skills *could* be made more congenial to the working of the local political system of the host society, but this would imply a drastic change in their lives and plans, with the paradoxical result that they would gain a real voice in the democratic process, but *not as migrants engaged in a temporary migration project*.

This takes us to the more general objection that our discussion misses the non-consequentialist, procedural and symbolic side of the argument from domination. In reply to this objection two things should be pointed out. First, the procedural requirement established by the non-domination principle cannot be a sham: if domination should be avoided, the parties involved need to have an actual opportunity to make their voice heard. We argue that this is not the case with the migrants engaged in temporary migration projects, because, given their life plans and conception of the good, the costs they would have to bear for achieving effective participation are disproportionately high if compared to those of the permanent residents' or of the migrants' who plan to stay; while for the latter achieving the social and cultural preconditions for effective political participation does not detract from the other plans and goals they may have in their lives, in the case of the migrants engaged in temporary migration projects such an achievement would entail an important deviation from the strategy set out as essential to carry out their plans. The unfairness of this arrangement clearly affects its procedural rightness.

The second point to make concerns the symbolic value of political rights. If we bear in mind the costs that the effective use of voting rights at the national level would imply for those temporary migrants who intend to return to their home country, we realize that granting them voting rights as the main tool for making their voice heard not only is unfair, but the mismatch between the institutional tools offered to these migrants and their actual existential condition amounts to a public misrecognition of the meaning and value of their life plans and of their decision to keep the centre of their lives in the country of origin. Whatever symbolic value the granting of voting rights may have, it is almost completely lost when it is premised on the misrecognition of the life plans of those involved.

Focusing on voting rights and enfranchisement in national elections as the most appropriate response to the vulnerability of the migrants engaged in temporary migration projects, therefore, is misguided not just because it is ineffective, but because of the specific reason why it is ineffective, i.e. that it fails to consider the special life plans of these migrants; by doing so, it does not fulfil the procedural requirements of the principle of non-domination and implies a symbolic misrecognition of these migrants.

Are there any better alternatives?

Focusing on voting rights at the national level as the most important and pressing claim to be made on behalf of temporary migrants is not only unfair to those migrants who are engaged in a temporary migration project, but also risks to detract attention from more efficient and procedurally appropriate ways to endow these migrants with political weight and effective channels for advocating their rights. We argue that the most promising alternative, in this respect, is mobilization through migrant non-governmental organizations, trade unions and migrant workers organisations.

Migrant non-governmental organizations have, of course, long been active in the service of migrants in different ways and with a variety of purposes. Some developments in this area are however of particular interest for our discussion here. As pointed out by an emerging literature, the last two decades have seen a number of new organizations developing in response to precariousness in the labour market that aim at achieving better conditions and protections for migrant workers through a series of strategies including advocacy, organizing migrant workers and training on rights (Heckscher and Carré 2006, Martin et al. 2007). Moreover, other migrant organizations that may not specifically identify as labour organizations have also been active in similar work, together with their more traditional role of service providers (Martin 2012) and advocates for a range of migrants' interests.

The most recent literature seems to also indicate that important changes are taking place that might highly increase unions' potential to become effective advocates of migrants' rights. Schmidt (2006) and Fitzgerald and Hardy (2010) list various ways in which national labour unions have changed their mode of operation in order to be more efficient in organizing temporary migrants: cooperation with unions in the country of origin (see also Meardi 2012); creation of regional or global migrant workers unions (Gordon and Turner 2000, Waddington 2000, Cotton and Gumbrell-McCormick 2012); portability of trade union membership across borders or mutual recognition of affiliations between national trade unions (Ford 2013, p. 263, Rosewarne 2013, p. 287); establishment of branches in the sending countries (Gordon 2007, p. 575); establishment of, or cooperation with, migrant worker centres that provide information, legal assistance and support to temporary migrant workers (Fine 2007, Choudry and Thomas 2013); and integration of migrants into national labour unions, sometimes involving derogations to strict equality among unionized workers, in order to make special provisions for temporary migrants.

Moreover, at least in some countries, unions have developed important forms of cooperation and synergy with migrant ethnic and national associations, migrant labour NGOs (Ford 2004, Oke 2012) and migrant grassroots movements (Hsia 2009). This last development is especially important, because through these interactions with NGOs and migrants' associations unions come to take into account the needs and interests of migrant workers in the informal sector (Piper 2013), and expand their area of advocacy also to rights and interests that do not strictly pertain to the workplace. Furthermore, counting on NGOs and grassroots movements may be important in dealing with migrants from, and to, countries where unions have been made illegal or have not been able to develop in suitable institutional forms (Ford 2009, Hsia 2009, Xu 2013). These developments seem to indicate that labour unions and migrant organizations may overcome the recruiting and advocacy difficulties that are evident in the case of political parties.

On the advocacy front, political parties, which have a national constituency and operate by the time frame fixed by national elections, have little incentive in becoming advocates of the rights of temporary migrants oriented to return. The same does not hold for unions and migrant organizations. These latter's interest in organizing and defending migrants is, of course, obvious, but also unions, unlike national political parties, may have a genuine transnational dimension; and even when they have an exclusively national dimension they may have an incentive to recruit and organize temporary migrants and defend their interests. In fact, it has been remarked that although national unions have traditionally been adverse to the liberalization of migration (Castles and Kosack 1973, Briggs 1998), once temporary migration has become a fait accompli, as it is now, they grow a pressing interest in organizing migrants, as an antidote to the social dumping and unfair competition that may come from the vexing contracts arranged by temporary work agencies (Watts 2002, Abella

2006, Schmidt 2006, Meardi 2012). Moreover, this interest in mobilizing migrants and defending their rights, although not completely exempt from the time frames of parliamentary and electoral politics, is not as dependent on them as the interest of parties and other national political organizations; also in this respect, therefore, unions are better suited to taking into account the interests of those migrants that cannot be counted upon as permanent residents or voters in the next elections.

Also on the recruitment front, unions and migrant organizations are better placed than parties. Unions are traditionally devoted not only to mobilizing workers, negotiating labour reforms and campaigning for labour rights, but also to providing individual workers with assistance and help with legal issues, tax forms and labour litigations. In relation to migrant workers, in recent years, they have been expanding the range of these activities and services, very often through the mediation and help of migrants' organizations and migrants' labour NGOs that traditionally already provide these services to migrants. For example, they started offering legal assistance with the visa and immigrant status, language courses, translation of legal documents and contracts, courses on safety at work, accommodation services, financial services and other forms of assistance that may make an important difference in the daily life of temporary migrants and respond to their most immediate interests and needs (Schmidt 2006, Heyes 2009, Fitzgerald and Hardy 2010). Even when these services are not conditional on joining unions, they serve as an important source of attraction for temporary migrants, and often provide the network and connections that may otherwise be lacking, especially when they are employed in jobs that keep them isolated, like, for example, live-in domestics (Ford and Piper 2007, Piper 2010, Holgate 2011).

These developments provide a factual basis for believing that migrant and labour organizations may be an effective means for giving voice to migrants who are oriented to return and protect their rights and interests. What is equally important from our perspective is that these forms of advocacy do not require, on the part of these migrants, inclusion in the host society or any deep engagement with its social and political system, although of course, the organizations themselves often need, and have, deep ties to the territory and extensive networks. Participation in them does not involve unfair costs for these migrants, who indeed can have immediate returns from joining without detracting from their long-term plans. At the same time, through their participation in organized labour those migrants who plan to return may still make their presence and weight visible and recognized within the host society. This means that not only representation through labour unions and migrants' organizations is fairer than representation through voting rights, but also that the symbolic function of representation is better performed by these means than by voting rights at the national level. Through these forms of representation migrants who move on a temporary basis acquire voice and visibility while retaining their social identity and status as foreigners who do not aim at inclusion; these forms of representation, therefore, do not involve a misrecognition of their special status and life projects.

Needless to say, for unions to perform this important function some important changes in the law and practice are required. For example, migrant temporary work agencies should be given incentives to provide information on unions to their members (and they should be subject to sanctions whenever they deter their workers from joining a union) (Schmidt 2006, Fitzgerald and Hardy 2010); membership in national unions should be made open to temporary residents (ILO 2004); and migrants' unions may need to be recognized as parties in the institutional system of labour negotiations of the host country. Furthermore, these transformations would be strongly facilitated by the recognition of fundamental civil and political rights for migrants, like the right of association and the right to form and join a trade union, which in many countries are denied to all workers, and in others are still denied to temporary workers, or are made insecure by the precariousness of the legal status of migrants under illiberal visa regimes (ILO 2010, p. 174). Some of these changes cannot be expected to happen quickly and smoothly. However, these issues of feasibility are not a reason for not pointing to labour unions and migrant workers' organizations as the most promising resource for giving voice to migrants engaged in temporary migration projects, especially in view of the fact that the changes that would be required in order to extend voting rights in the host countries to these migrants might be even more unfeasible and controversial.

The effects on democratic institutions

Concentrating our attention on unions and migrant organizations is the most effective way to provide migrants engaged in temporary migration projects with a political voice as well as remedying their particular vulnerabilities and recognizing their life plans. There is however also a more general concern about the effects that this type of migration or circular and temporary migration in general, may have on democratic institutions.

Such concern, as Bauböck (2011) has argued, becomes evident once we seriously consider the possible consequences for democratic institutions of a sustained and numerically significant flow of temporary migration, a migration that, by its very nature, does not tend towards the full integration of migrants in the host societies. He paints for us a picture of a dystopic world of hypermigration, as he calls it, where the majority of the people present at any time in any given territory are not permanent residents, nor necessarily citizens of the country they momentarily find themselves in. In this situation, Bauböck argues, intergenerational territorially based citizenship would cease to make sense, and would necessarily be replaced by a *ius soli* citizenship, understood as a strict principle of territoriality, with people taking up and leaving their citizenship as easily and frequently as they change their domicile. Bauböck warns us that much of value would be lost in this transformation, for he believes birthright membership in political communities to be not only morally defensible, but also functionally required for stable, substantively self-determining political communities.

This thought experiment helps us think through the implications of what Bauböck argues is temporary migrants' condition of partial citizenship. Temporary migrants are, in this line of argument, partial citizens in both host and home societies. In the country of origin, they are partial citizens because their absence from the territory must necessarily mean their citizenship is diminished. Countries of origin, Bauböck argues, must grant their temporary emigrants a whole range of rights, including vote by absentee ballot. But in territorially bounded polities 'residence inevitably makes a difference' with regard to the rights attached to citizenship. In the host county, as long as citizenship is understood as a bounded, stable and intergenerational status, migrants' very condition of temporariness, if they are foreign nationals, means they are not full citizens by definition, nor are they on the road to full citizenship as there is no expectation of permanence.

It is unclear however, whether the picture of partial citizenship painted by Bauböck applies to migrants engaged in temporary migration projects. In fact, as we have argued, temporary migration projects are characterized precisely by the fact that the life of the migrants engaged in them centres in the country of origin. Migrants remain in touch with their home society and may find various ways of still participating in the life of their country even if from afar. Moreover, their interests, their future and their life plans are located in the country of origin, giving them a real and clear stake in their society's future. The picture of uprootedness painted by Bauböck seems therefore to not apply to them, even though it may constitute a problem in a future possible world of hypermigration.

On the side of the host country, the idea of partial citizenship is in fact an inappropriate description of the position of migrants engaged in temporary migration projects. This definition misrepresents the migrants' own understanding of their migratory experience as a temporary one and of its role in their overall life plans. The institutional means to their political participation should recognize this and provide forms of participation that are instrumental to the protection of needs and interests specific to these migratory experiences rather than forms of incorporation that tend to full inclusion. This is precisely what transnational trade unions and migrant associations could achieve for migrants engaged in temporary migration projects. If an appropriate institutional regime is provided to accommodate these migratory experiences, their presence within the host country will not be problematic for liberal democratic institutions, which are indeed weakened and corrupted by the presence of partial citizens, but not by the presence of appropriately and fully recognized temporary 'members'.

There is however, a situation that may arise from temporary migration projects where the concerns that Bauböck highlights are indeed real dangers. As we have argued, these projects are often highly risky pursuits in which migrants may find themselves trapped. This may happen because return has become too costly due to loss of opportunities or disrupted relationships in the home country. Migrants who find themselves in this position will indeed suffer from a condition of partial citizenship. This represents a problem not only for the migrants but also for the democratic institutions of the host country which cannot tolerate such lack of enfranchisement.

It is to be noted that often current institutional settings function precisely to increase the risk of entrapment because they fail to support the migrants' plan of return, and either insist on applying traditional forms of incorporation for temporary migrants or, in the case of temporary migration programs, make it harder for the migrants to succeed at their project by instituting limitations to their freedoms – e.g. lack of freedom to move, visa restrictions that ties the particular migrant to a specific employer increasing the risk of exploitation, etc. – but also directly impact the migrants' capacity to maintain relationships with their home country – e.g. lack of possibility to travel back and forth which becomes disruptive of family relations. These limbo situations however, are also directly addressed by our suggestion of special rights whose function would in part be precisely to provide exit options for migrants, either to aid the successful attainment of the migrants' aims, therefore facilitating returns, or to provide pathways towards full integration and permanency in the host community.

Conclusion

We have argued that the powerful arguments that liberal political theorists make for the full inclusion of migrants in the receiving communities is mis-guided in the case of those migrants engaged in temporary migration projects. These migrants never intend to move permanently to the receiving country but rather intend their migration to be a specific temporary step within a larger life plan, whose aims centre around the home country. As a consequence, these migrants tend not to invest in integrating within the host country. This particu-lar migratory experience therefore needs recognition and accommodation not through traditional inclusion within the host society but rather through a set of special rights that have a good fit with the migrants' aims. We have argued that this holds also for proposals aimed at granting temporary migrants political rights in the host country and suggested instead that unions and migrants' labour organizations are a better response to ensure the possibility of political participation and voice for migrants engaged in temporary migration projects. This ensures their own protection but also respect for democratic principles and the health of liberal democratic institutions which are always endangered by the existence of a class of people who are subject to the laws of the country but do not have political voice.

Notes

1. Claiming that many migrants aim at temporary rather than permanent migration does not imply that the current revival of 'temporary migration programs' (Castles 2006) is congenial to this type of migratory plans. Besides their often exploitative and demeaning character (Basok 2004, Carens 2008, Anderson 2010, Lenard and Strahele 2012), these programs are usually designed to serve the labour market of the receiving country, rather than the plans of migrants. This means, for example, that many of them may be forced to return at a time that is highly unsuited to their overall plans (Dustmann 2003).
2. When return is successful, migrants express satisfaction with their migratory experience despite the undeniable sacrifices it entails. For example, in a study of return migration to the Maghreb area Collier, Piracha, and Randazzo find that 79.5% of the return migrants they interviewed asserted they had obtained advantages from their period overseas, and 38% hoped to repeat the experience (Collier *et al.* 2011).
3. Clear examples of social rights that presume stability are the pension system and public schools.
4. See Walzer (1983), Bauböck (2009), Rubio-Marin (2000).
5. On this we agree with Sager and depart from other recent discussions of domination in relation to non-citizen residents (Benton 2014, Hovdal-Moan 2014).

References

Abella, M., 2006. Policies and best practices for the management of temporary migration. *Paper presented at the international symposium on international migration and development*, 28–30 June, Turin: United Nations Secretariat.

Aleman-Castilla, B., 2007. *The returns to temporary migration to the United States: evidence from the Mexican urban employment survey.* Discussion paper no. 804. London: Center for Economic Performance.

Alexandru, M., 2007. Migration and social mobility. A new perspective on status inconsistency. *Romanian journal of European studies*, 5–6, 153–167.

Anderson, B., 2010. Migration, immigration controls and the fashioning of precarious workers. *Work, employment & society*, 24, 300–317.

Anghel, R.G., 2013. *Romanians in Western Europe: migration, status dilemmas, and transnational connections.* Lanham, MD: Lexington Books.

Basok, T., 2004. Postnational citizenship, social exclusion and migrants rights: Mexican seasonal workers in Canada. *Citizenship Studies*, 8, 47–64.

Bauböck, R., 2009. Stakeholder citizenship and democratic participation in migrant contexts. *In*: J.E. Fossum, J. Poirier and P. Magnette, eds. *The ties that bind: accommodating diversity in canada and the European Union.* Brussels: Peter Lang, 105–128.

Bauböck, R., 2011. Temporary migrants, partial citizenship and hypermigration. *Critical review of international social and political philosophy*, 14, 665–693.

Bauer, T. and Gang, I.N., 1998. *Temporary migrants from Egypt: how long do they stay abroad?* Institute for the Study of Labour discussion paper no. 3. Available from: http://ideas.repec.org/p/iza/izadps/dp3.html [Accessed 20 July 2013].

Benton, S., 2014. The problem of denizenship: a non-domination framework. *Critical review of international social and political philosophy*, 17, 49–69.

van den Berg, G.J. and Weynandt, M.A., 2012. *Explaining differences between the expected and actual duration until return migration: economic changes.* SOEP papers on multidisciplinary panel data research, no. 497.

Black, R., Engbersen, G., Okolski, M., and Pantiru, C., eds., 2010. *A continent moving West? EU enlargement and labour migration from Central and Eastern Europe.* Amsterdam: Amsterdam University Press.

Briggs, V.J., 1998. Income disparity and unionism: the workplace influences of post-1995 immigration policy. *In*: J.A. Auerbach and R.S. Belous, eds. *The inequality paradox: growth of income disparity.* Washington, DC: National Policy Association, 112–132.

Carens, J.H., 2008. Live-in domestics, seasonal workers, and others hard to locate on the map of democracy. *Journal of political philosophy*, 16 (4), 419–445.

Castagnone, E., Eve, M., Petrillo, E.R., and Piperno, F. 2007. *Madri migranti* [Migrant mothers], CeSpi working papers, 37/2007. Roma: CeSpi.

Castles, S., 2006. Guestworkers in Europe: a resurrection? *International migration review*, 40 (4), 741–766.

Castles, S. and Kosack, G., 1973. *Immigrant workers and class structure in Western Europe.* Oxford: Oxford University Press.

Catania, D., Recchia, D., Simoni, M., and Zucca, G., 2007. *'Il welfare fatto in casa'. Indagine nazionale sui collaboratori domestici stranieri che lavorano a sostegno delle famiglie italiane* [Home-made welfare. National inquiry on foreign domestic workers aiding Italian families]. Roma: Iref.

Chaloupek, G. and Peyrl, J., 2009. EU labour migration: government and social partner policies in Austria. *In*: B. Galgoczi, J. Leschke, and A. Watt, eds. *EU labour migration since enlargement.* Aldershot: Ashgate, 171–184.

Choudry, A. and Thomas, M., 2013. Labour struggle for workplace justice: migrant and immigrant worker organizing in Canada. *Journal of industrial relations*, 55 (2), 212–226.

Collier, W., Piracha, M., and Randazzo, T., 2011. *Remittances and return migration.* IZA Discussion paper no. 6091. Available from: http://ssrn.com/abstract=1958747 [Accessed 4 August 2013].

Cotton, E. and Gumbrell-McCormick, R., 2012. Global unions as imperfect multilateral organizations. *Economic and industrial democracy*, 33 (4), 707–728.

Dustmann, C., 1996. Return migration: the European experience. *Economic policy*, 11, 213–250.

Dustmann, C., 2003. Return migration, wage differentials, and the optimal migration duration. *European economic review*, 47 (2), 353–367.

Dustmann, C. and Weiss, Y., 2007. *Return migration: theory and empirical evidence.* CReAM discussion paper 02/07. London, CReAM.

European Commission, Directorate-General for Economic and Financial affairs, 2009. *Five years of an enlarged EU, 1/2009.* Luxembourg: Office for Official Publications of the European Communities.

Fedyuk, O., 2012. Images of transnational motherhood: the role of photographs in measuring time and maintaining connections between Ukraine and Italy. *Journal of ethnic and migration studies*, 38 (2), 279–300.

Fihel, A. and Grabowska-Lusinska, I., 2014. Labour market behaviours of back-and-forth migrants from Poland. *International migration*, 52 (1), 22–35.

Fine, J., 2007. A marriage made in heaven? Mismatches and misunderstandings between worker centres and unions. *British journal of industrial relations*, 45 (2), 335–360.

Fitzgerald, I. and Hardy, J., 2010. Thinking outside the box: trade union organizing strategies and polish migrant workers in the United Kingdom. *British journal of industrial relations*, 48 (1), 131–150.

Ford, M., 2004. Organizing the unorganizable: unions, NGOs, and Indonesian migrant labour. *International migration*, 42 (5), 99–119.

Ford, M., 2009. *Workers and intellectuals: NGOs, trade unions and the Indonesian labour movement*. Singapore: National University of Singapore Press.

Ford, M., 2013. The Global Union Federations and temporary labour migration in Malaysia. *Journal of industrial relations*, 55 (2), 260–276.

Ford, M. and Piper, N., 2007. Southern sites of female agency. *In*: J.M. Hobson and L. Seabrooke, eds. *Everyday politics of the world economy*. Cambridge: Cambridge University Press, 63–80.

Fouron, G., 2003. Haitian immigrants in the United States. *In*: B.S.A. Yeoh, M.W. Charney, and T.C. Kiong, eds. *Approaching transnationalisms*. Boston, MA: Kluwer, 205–250.

Glystos, N.P., 1997. Remitting behaviour of 'temporary' and 'permanent' migrants: the case of Greeks in Germany and Australia. *Labour*, 11, 409–435.

Gordon, J., 2007. Transnational labor citizenship. *Southern California law review*, 80, 503–588.

Gordon, M.E. and Turner, L., 2000. *Transnational cooperation among labor unions*. Ithaca, NY: Cornell University Press.

Hammar, T., 1990. *Democracy and the nation state*. Aldershot: Gower.

Heckscher, C. and Carré, F., 2006. Strength in networks: employment rights organizations and the problem of co-ordination. *British journal of industrial relations*, 44 (4), 605–628.

Heyes, J., 2009. Recruiting and organising migrant workers through education and training: a comparison of community and the GMB. *Industrial relations journal*, 40 (3), 182–197.

Holgate, J., 2011. Temporary migrant workers and labor organization. *Working USA: the journal of labor and society*, 14, 191–199.

Hovdal-Moan, M., 2014. Unequal residence statuses and the ideal of non-domination. *Critical review of international social and political philosophy*, 17 (1), 70–89.

Hsia, H., 2009. The making of a transnational grassroots migrant movement. *Critical Asian studies*, 41 (1), 113–141.

Hugo, G., 2009. Circular migration and development. *In*: O. Hofírek, R. Klvanová, and M. Nekorjak, eds. *Boundaries in motion: rethinking contemporary migration events*. Brno: Centre for the Study of Democracy and Culture (CDK), 165–190.

ILO, 2004. *Towards a fair deal for migrant workers in the global economy*. Geneva: International Labour Office.

ILO, 2010. *International labour migration. A rights-based approach*. Geneva: Author.

Kostakopoulou, D., 2008. *The future governance of citizenship*. New York: Cambridge University Press.

Lenard, P., 2012. Democratic self-determination and non-citizen residents. *Comparative sociology*, 11, 649–669.

Lenard, P. and Strahele, C., 2012. Temporary labour migration, global redistribution, and democratic justice. *Politics, philosophy and economics*, 11 (2), 206–230.

Leogrande, A., 2008. *Uomini e caporali: viaggio tra i nuovi schiavi nelle campagne del sud* [Men and foremen: a journey among the new slaves in the Southern countryside of Italy]. Milano: Mondadori.

Martin, N., Morales, S., and Theodore, N., 2007. Migrant worker centers: contending with downgrading in the low-wage labor market. *GeoJournal*, 68 (2–3), 155–165.

Martin, N., 2012. There is abuse everywhere: migrant nonprofit organizations and the problem of precarious work. *Urban affairs review*, 48 (3), 389–416.

Meardi, G., 2012. Union immobility? Trade unions and the freedoms of movement in the enlarged EU. *British journal of industrial relations*, 50 (1), 99–120.

OECD, 2008. *International migration outlook annual report*. Paris: Organisation for Economic Co-operation and Development.

Oke, N., 2012. Temporary migration, transnational politics? *Journal of intercultural studies*, 33 (1), 85–101.

Ottonelli, V. and Torresi, T., 2012. Inclusivist egalitarian liberalism and temporary migration: a dilemma. *Journal of political philosophy*, 20 (2), 202–224.

Ottonelli, V. and Torresi, T., 2013. When is migration voluntary? *International migration review*, 47 (4), 783–813.

Parreñas, R.S., 2001. *Servants of globalization. Women, migration and domestic work*. Stanford: Stanford University Press.

Piper, N., 2010. Temporary economic migration and rights activism: an organizational perspective. *Ethnic and racial studies*, 33 (1), 108–125.

Piper, N., 2013. Resisting inequality. The rise of global migrant rights activism. *In*: T. Bastia, ed. *Migration and inequality*. New York: Routledge, 45–64.

Piracha, M. and Vadean, F., 2009. *Return migration and occupational choice*. Department of Economics discussion paper 09/05. Canterbury: University of Kent.

Rawls, J., 1993. *Political liberalism*. New York: Columbia University Press.

Rosewarne, S., 2013. The internationalisation of construction capital and labour force formation. *Journal of industrial relations*, 55 (2), 277–297.

Rubio-Marin, R., 2000. *Immigration as a democratic challenge*. New York: Cambridge University Press.

Sager, A., 2014. Political rights, republican freedom, and temporary workers. *Critical review of international social and political philosophy*, 17 (2), 189–211.

Schmidt, V., 2006. *Merchants of labour*. Geneva: International Institute for Labour Studies.

Schroeder, D. and Gefenas, E., 2009. Vulnerability: too vague and too broad. *Cambridge quarterly of healthcare ethics*, 18 (2), 113–121.

Stark, O., 1991. *The migration of labor*. Oxford: Blackwell.

Stoll, M.A. and Wong, J.S., 2007. Immigration and civic participation in a multiracial and multiethnic context. *International migration review*, 41, 880–908.

Tsuda, T., 2013. Return migration and ethnicity. *In*: I. Ness, ed. *The encyclopaedia of global human migration*. Oxford: Wiley-Blackwell. http://onlinelibrary.wiley.com/doi/10.1002/9781444351071.wbeghm454/full [Accessed August 2013].

Uccellini, C.M., 2010. Outsiders after Accession: the case of Romanian migrants in Italy, 1989–2009. *Political perspectives*, 4 (2), 70–85.

Vadean F.P. and Piracha, M., 2009. *Circular migration or permanent return: what determines different forms of migration?* IZA discussion papers, No. 4287. Available from: http://nbn-resolving.de/urn:nbn:de:101:1-2009082190 [Accessed 4 August 2013].

Waddington, J., 2000. Towards a reform agenda? European trade unions in transition. *Industrial relations journal*, 31 (4), 317–330.

Walzer, M., 1983. *Spheres of justice*. New York: Basic Books.

Watts, J.R., 2002. *Immigration policy and the challenge of globalization. Unions and employers in unlikely alliance.* Ithaca, NY: Cornell Univesity Press.

Xu, Y., 2013. Labor non-governmental organizations in China: mobilizing rural migrant workers. *Journal of industrial relations*, 55 (2), 243–259.

Detaining immigrants and asylum seekers: a normative introduction

Stephanie J. Silverman

Refugee Research Network, Centre for Refugee Studies, York University, Toronto, Canada

Detention of irregular migrants and asylum seekers takes place at the behest and convenience of virtually all liberal states. It is a harmful practice that impacts non-citizens as well as citizens, and has far-reaching ramifications for our understandings of the ethics of immigration and border control. Thus far, however, normative theorists engaged in the vibrant immigration admissions debate have remained mostly silent on the topic of detention. By unmasking and revealing the essential roles played by detention in enforcing immigration controls, this paper is intended to highlight the dangers for normative theory of maligning or underestimating detention. In particular, a study of detention refocuses scholarly attention on the temporal and spatial aspects of immigration enforcement, the undesirability of warehousing or containment proposals for addressing refugee or immigration crises, and the virtually irreconcilable ethical conflicts at the core of the immigration admissions debate. Normative theorists would be remiss in ignoring the ethical and practical consequences for an increasingly large number of people that are exacted by detention practices worldwide.

Introduction

Liberal states are continuously expanding the detention systems that incarcerate irregular migrants and asylum seekers. At its base, detention is the policy or practice of depriving someone of his or her liberty because of citizenship status. It is not always possible to recognise detention when it is occurring. This is because detention centres are disguised under different names, including immigration removal centres (UK), immigration holding centres (Canada), *centres de rétention administrative* (France), foreigners' guesthouses (Turkey), and service processing centres and contract detention facilities (USA). Detention is the unmentioned or disguised foundation undergirding a number of short-term or intermediate 'solutions' to refugee or immigration crises supported by liberals and liberal states.

The significance of detention is often repudiated by discounting it as a minor component of the more important issue of border control and migrant selection. Despite this presentation, detention is known to harm people, and not just immigrant detainees. Certainly, research demonstrates that detention inflicts lifelong damages on the mental and physical well-being of detainees. In addition, however, it impacts detainees' networks, including their loved ones and advocates; it burdens citizens with the fiscal costs of its financial upkeep, and with the insecurity and suspicion that having prison-like structures built may convey; and it destabilises communities through the effects of making non-citizens aware of their constant vulnerability to detention and other enforcement measures.[1] As detention of migrants continues to increase in scope and scale across almost every liberal state, the significance to normative theory of its key component of deprivation of liberty based on citizenship status cannot be underestimated.

It is pertinent to unmask some of the ethical concerns raised by detention and to encourage discussion of these points by normative theorists who are already engaged in the immigration admissions debate. This article is not focused on a state's right to control immigration across its borders, but rather on the exercise and recognition of this right when it is deployed.

This article begins with a brief study of the immigration admissions debate in normative theory. This study presages an overview of the rise of detention and its key moral dilemmas: in particular, how deprivation of liberty is an affront to the basic human rights – including the right to freedom – that liberal states are committed to protecting. Next, the paper interrogates the conventional justification for detention – a need to prevent absconding – and finds that it is only partially plausible. The paper then turns to examine why normative theorists have been relatively silent on detention. Of concern here is the mislabelling and mischaracterisation of detention found in the 'warehousing' or 'containment' of asylum seekers and refugees in the Global South. Miller's (2005) proposal for the creation of 'safety zones' is analysed as an initially promising but ultimately problematic solution to the uncertainties of immediate refugee resettlement. The paper concludes by highlighting three insights from the normative evaluation of detention practices, which identify weaknesses in the standard understandings of admission and exclusion described by normative theorists participating in the immigration admissions debate.

Detention and normative ethics: an overview

An increasing number of normative theorists are engaging in a thoughtful discussion on who to admit (and exclude), and when and why these decisions may or may not be morally acceptable. This wide-ranging discussion can be termed the *immigration admissions debate*. Using Oberman's (2009) terminology, there are, generally speaking, two sides in the immigration admissions debate: (i) 'border control defenders' who do not see the exclusion from membership rights of non-citizens without special claims as, in itself, unjust; and (ii) 'free movement advocates' arguing that justice demands a significant easing of current immigration restrictions. Wilcox (2009, p. 813) suggests that the 'conventional view' on immigration admissions falls more on the side of the border control defenders: liberal states 'will typically admit immigrants whose talents, assets, characteristics, or skills are perceived to be in the national interest, but they are morally free to restrict immigration as they see fit, with few exceptions'.

Yet, these debates pay no attention to the practice of detaining migrants as they attempt to cross borders and gain admission. This is a significant over-sight: Immigration detention plays an essential role in controlling the border and enforcing immigration policy. Not only is detention a stand-alone practice, but it is implicated in the functioning of any robust system of immigration control. In this way, detention has grown to become interdependent with immigration enforcement policy and practice in all liberal states.

As a non-entrée and pre-deportation practice, detention may be targeted against nationals of many different states, or nationals of a particular state. Liberal state governments are consistently detaining people for more immigration-related reasons and for longer periods of time than ever before (Silverman 2013, p. 1). Most developed detention systems include not only the detention centres themselves but also a number of reporting centres, transit centres, short-term holding facilities near airports and seaports, and prison cells. They may also include informal holding areas such as hotel rooms, airplane hangars, and buses or other transport vehicles. What these facilities all share is a focus on restraining the movements and freedoms of migrants, who are often portrayed as violating the state's right to determine admission. Upon release, former detainees are frequently asked to wear ankle bracelets, adhere to reporting requirements, and be home for curfews and on-site visits. These policies restrain the movements of migrants as immigration officials consider their cases further.

In legal terms, immigration detention is ordinarily understood as an administrative process meant to aid in an orderly and efficient adjudication of immigrant and refugee claims (Clayton 2006, p. 510). Despite detention centres often resembling prisons, the practice cannot legally be used to punish migrants and asylum seekers. With the exception of those states that have legislated for mandatory incarceration of some groups, detention is a discretionary power exercised by immigration officials. There are international legal rules that detention should be for the shortest time possible and treated as a 'last resort'.

In states such as the UK and the USA, there are no official time limits on detention. Typically, lengths of detention span two to six months in the UK detention estate. Over the period December 2008–December 2010, approximately 10% of UK immigration detainees were held between six months and one year, and an additional 8–10% were held in excess of one year

(Silverman 2011, p. 3). Case law has managed to establish an extreme upper limit of six years of pre-deportation immigration detention (Wilsher 2008, pp. 905–906). In the USA, 4 out of every 10 detainees are held for less than three days and about 70% experience less than one month of detention (Transactional Records Access Clearinghouse [TRAC] 2013). While the 2008 European Union *Returns Directive* recommends a maximum stay of six months of pre-removal detention with an optional 12-month extension, the UK has declined to implement this recommendation. Then again, the *Directive* would not provide a panacea for detention in the UK and across Europe because it allows for substantial deprivation of liberty without routine judicial oversight. Further, many European states have now set time limits of *under* 18 months, including, for example, France (one and a half months), the Netherlands (one and a half months), Spain (two months) and Italy (six months) (Bhui 2013, p. 24).

In the USA and the UK, most immigration detainees are arrested when trying to enter the country without prior, official authorisation, or upon discovery that they have been residing without the appropriate documents. In these instances, detention facilitates identification, status determination, and, potentially, deportation of non-citizens. The official reasons for a person's detention can shift even though (i) the detainee is not moved; (ii) the detainee and his or her solicitor are not notified; or (iii) nothing in the detainee's claims for admissions have changed. For example, a detainee could be originally detained for overstaying a visa but then be held while his or her subsequently lodged asylum claim is being adjudicated (Silverman 2013, pp. 175–176). Detention efforts are also central to a number of extraterritorial measures that interdict, or stop, migrants from reaching destination states by apprehending them and sending them to temporary protection in *third-country processing centres* and/ or *regional protection areas*.

Scandals over detention can cause serious disruption to an immigration enforcement bureaucracy. The UK case is instructive here. The landmark 1998 White Paper, *Fairer, Faster and Firmer – A Modern Approach to Immigration and Asylum*, stipulates that detention is normally justified where: (i) there is a reasonable belief that the individual will fail to keep the terms of temporary admission or temporary release; (ii) initially, a person's identity and the basis of his or her claim needs to be clarified; or (iii) removal is imminent. In particular, detention is justified 'where there is a systematic attempt to breach the immigration control' system (UK Home Office 1998, Paragraph 12.3). Yet, this system was fundamentally changed after the April 2006 revelations that 160 foreign nationals were released from prison into the UK despite orders from courts recommending their removal, with 20 of these post-sentence detainees subsequently re-convicted of 'more serious' offences after their release.[2] The public backlash following the scandal led to the resignation of the Home Secretary and, eventually, the 2007 UK Borders Act. Under the 2007 Act, all non-European Economic Area (EEA) citizens sentenced to 12 months custody or more face mandatory detention before deportation unless their removal breaches international obligations, while EEA citizens will be detained and then deported if they are sentenced to 24 months custody (BBC World Service 2006, Bosworth 2011, p. 3, Silverman 2013, p. 108).

Detention is costly in many ways. It requires the cooperation of a diverse array of public actors – such as doctors, nurses, social workers, police officers, therapists, immigration judges and pro bono lawyers. Governments contract with private actors such as maintenance and landscaping companies, catering companies, private security firms, and detainee escort providers. The remarkable level of involvement from private prison firms eager to participate in the detention sphere is documented in the literature exploring the 'immigration industrial complex' (e.g. Golash-Boza 2009, Díaz 2011, Gammeltoft-Hansen and Sørensen 2012, Trujillo-Pagan 2013). It is not surprising that detention has attracted such a high degree of attention from private firms looking for a profit: The UK detention estate costs £120 (about $191 USD) per person per day and the US estate costs up to $166 USD (about £103) per detainee per day with the entire US estate costing out at $1.9 billion USD (about £1.18 billion) annually (Silverman 2013, pp. 1–2).

Detention is known to impact negatively the mental well-being of both adults and children. The open-ended nature of immigration detention in states where there are no time limits is particularly damaging. Detainees present higher levels of suicide and self-harm than the prison population (McGinley and Trude 2012, p. 4). Psychological distress indicators amongst detainees often include 'depression, suicidal ideation, posttraumatic stress, anxiety, panic, and physical symptoms', particularly when 'compared with compatriot asylum seekers, refugees, and immigrants living in the community' (Silove et al. 2000, p. 608). Child detainees, in particular, are 'clearly vulnerable, marginalized, and at risk of mental and physical harm as a result of state sanctioned neglect (inadequate care and protection), and possibly abuse in the sense of exposure to violence within the detention facilities themselves' (Lorek et al. 2009, p. 584). The deleterious effects on detainees' mental and physical health persist for years after release, and can have lifelong effects on children's cognitive and emotional development (Physicians for Human Rights and The Bellevue/NYU Program for Survivors of Torture 2003, p. 5, Steel et al. 2006).

The liberal commitment to freedom

A key value in liberal democracies is respect for personal freedom, understood as the right to personal liberty. Having and exercising 'control over our bodies, and in particular being protected against unwanted interference by others, is important to our sense of ourselves as human agents' (Miller 2012, p. 418). Deprivation of liberty is therefore 'the most invasive power that the state possesses' (Young 1991, p. 329).

Respect for liberty is fundamental to liberalism.[3] Yet, the right to personal liberty has never been absolute: for example, states often legitimately use deprivation of liberty to fight crime and maintain security (Kessler 2008–2009, p. 580). However, freedom from *arbitrary* arrest or detention is so important to be enshrined as a cornerstone in state constitutions (Hirschl 2000) and conventions of international law (Kessler 2008–2009). Arbitrary or disproportionate uses of detention are seen as 'non-compensable and unjust deprivations' of liberty and can 'shatter our tenuous sense of autonomy and self-determination' (Young 1991, p. 329). The right to be free from arbitrary detention usually translates in law to an obligation on states to provide procedural protections for individuals during arrests and detentions.

Cases of detention cannot be arbitrary or disproportionate, or they risk being considered illegal acts. The key European judgements on the legality of detention[4] together highlight that immigration detention is not prima facie arbitrary, provided that deportation is being pursued with 'due diligence' (Costello 2012, p. 281). Detention that is excessively long or viewed as arbitrary risks violating this due diligence rule (Hailbronner 2007, pp. 165, 172).

Yet, it is legally and normatively difficult to define and apply both the due diligence rule and a threshold at which detention becomes arbitrary. For example, periods of detention can be arbitrary on account of their (extended) lengths, which would presumably violate the due diligence rule. However, according to the European Court of Human Rights, as long as detention is considered to be serving a legitimate public interest, it cannot be considered arbitrary (Hailbronner 2007, p. 169); this understanding challenges the time limits question. In other words, it is problematic to pin down when immigration officials are – or, more importantly, are *not* – undertaking the appropriate steps to arrange for repatriation to a sending state. While the authority to detain is not at issue here, what is questionable is the exercise of this authority when rescinding liberty rights becomes arbitrary, and, hence, normatively impermissible.

The absconding concern

Stated aims for detention include ensuring cooperation with immigration officials and realising deportation of people with no right to stay (Costello and Kaytaz 2013, p. 7); however, it seems that a motivation to prevent absconding underwrites and animates the justification for the entire detention enterprise. Acts of absconding represent a loss of contact with non-citizens, and this loss undermines the state's ability to enforce immigration rules, administer its borders, and exercise its sovereign right to territorial control (Silverman 2013, pp. 100–101). From an empirical perspective, absconding represents a diminution of power, security, and oversight, which, normatively speaking, subverts the state's moral authority to the monopoly of control over migration.

Absconding can be understood as living in the territory of a state without authorisation and deliberately losing contact with the immigration authorities (Griffiths 2010, p. 3). The International Detention Coalition defines absconding as '[a]ctions taken by an individual to avoid contact with immigration authorities in order to avoid legal migration proceedings and outcomes' (Sampson *et al.* 2011, p. 3). The act of absconding also occurs when a non-citizen purposely does not comply with removal orders or refuses to register with immigration authorities.

The empirical data on absconding – while potentially biased as it is collected mainly by NGOs – indicates that high compliance or cooperation rates can be achieved *without* custodial detention. The keys to successful non-custodial measures are case management, supervision, information, and advice (Crépeau 2012, p. 13). For instance, between February 1997 and March 2000, the Vera Institute of Justice in New York City ran the Appearance Assistance Program as a non-custodial immigration enforcement measure. Vera found that (i) close community supervision is a practical possibility, even in a large metropolitan centre; (ii) community supervision will increase the efficiency of the expensive detention system; and (iii) that most irregular immigrants and asylum seekers 'want to comply, and that good supervision more than makes up for any deterrent impact that the possibility of immediate re-detention might have' (Stone 2000, p. 686, *passim*). Virtually all non-custodial programmes report that people without the right to stay but who are living in family units, particularly those with children, are unlikely to abscond. This is because parents are wary of withdrawing children from the health and educational services in which they are embedded while living in a liberal state (Crawley 2011, p. 1). These non-custodial measures not only cost less than conventional detention but also allow the enrollees to live in dignity until removal dates are reached (Silverman 2013, pp. 102, 131).

Moreover, even when people do abscond from immigration authorities, there is often a normatively justifiable reason for doing so. Plausible, rational reasons for absconding include: the mental trauma of impending or continuing detention; additional financial, emotional or other dependence on the irregular migrant or asylum seeker; and the need to visit and care for sick or needy family or friends (Silverman 2013, p. 114). These reasons are borne out in real life, including in a study by members of the Jesuit Refugee Service who were able to contact a number of absconders. The NGO discovered that absconding was driven by 'elements of fear – fear of return, destitution, being unable to provide for oneself and the family and loss of personal dignity' (Jesuit Refugee Service – Europe 2011, p. 7). Absconders also 'cited the need to work and earn money as a primary reason' for falling off an immigration enforcement radar (ibid.). Liberal state governments such as the UK and the USA are increasingly unwilling to provide an adequate standard of living because they are refusing to open up access to social welfare benefits or the right to work. Accordingly, these states are complicit in fostering a collective desire amongst non-citizens to abscond, and, thus, in fuelling the immigration detention estate.

The collective data demonstrates that non-citizens with pending immigration cases have vested interests in *not* absconding. The fact that they generally do *not* abscond challenges the logical motivation for detention practices in liberal states. Further, when contextualised with the liberal commitment to free-dom, the normative rationalisation for detention based on risk of absconding becomes even more flimsy. The potential benefits of preventing a minority of people from absconding are not significant enough to balance or outweigh the harms that detention causes to detainees, their networks and the wider political community. Further normative questions about absconding are bracketed for now, and the next section of the paper will explore the contours of justifying detention.

Accounting for the silence of normative theorists

The significant normative dilemma emerging from this discussion of the severe degree of the restrictions on a detainee's liberty rights and the inconsistency of the justifications for liberal states' practices of detention is clear to see. Yet, despite the harms caused by the practice, detention has not attracted a great deal of attention from normative theorists. Given that scholars of crimmigration studies,[5] as well as those developing Giorgio Agamben's *state of exception*,[6] are actively investigating the implications of the expanding worldwide regime of detention practices for their fields of study, this relative silence from norma-tive theorists is puzzling.

There are at least four explanations for this relative lack of attention, with the first three being practically minded.[7] First, the rapid expansion of detention of irregular immigrants and asylum seekers has taken place relatively recently. In the UK, for example, detention has grown from a comparatively small estate in the early 1990s to amongst the largest in Europe by the end of the 2000s. It takes time for scholarship to address phenomena that evolve as quickly as detention has. Second, the complexities of detention make it difficult to approach analytically. It is cumbersome to identify a universal definition of immigration detention. Further, immigration detention typically takes place within and outside the state's territorial jurisdiction as well as along its borders in a variety of buildings and under a number of guises. It can last for long periods of time, has unpredictable results, and is governed by a disparate vari-ety of legal cases and legislation that are being constantly challenged and refashioned. Detention's fluid and contentious nature does not lend itself to rapid comprehension or framework building.

Third, following from the insight that detention is tricky to pin down con-ceptually, an ethical-political vocabulary to discuss the practice is also elusive. The conceptual equating of barriers to admission with border enforcement con-centrates scholarly interest on issues of asylum, deportation, *non-refoulement*, and the like. Detention refocuses attention on the *shifting* border, one described by Shachar (2007, p. 193) as 'a complex, multilayered, and ever-transforming border, one that is drawn and redrawn, through the words of law and acts of regulatory agencies, to better caliber the admitting state's exclusion lines in response to new global challenges'. Bringing detention into the analysis requires rethinking how we speak about membership, state sovereignty, and the liberty rights of individuals.

The fourth reason that could explain why normative theorists have not turned to examining detention in great numbers may be linked to the practice's normative complexity. Such a discussion would necessarily be nested within a larger analytic framework focussed on the immigration admissions debate. After all, as Laegaard (2010, p. 252), argues,

> any discussion about how restrictive the immigration policy of a state should be presupposes that the state in principle has the right to exclude immigrants; if the state did not have such a right, the only permissible policy would be one of open borders.

The normative puzzles of detention connect to a fundamental tension in the political and ethical principles of liberal statehood: namely, the principle of impartial, universal equality that would seem to demand open borders is in normative conflict with the principle of popular sovereignty (and its corollary, the principle of self-determination) that mandates collective control, without interference, over the affairs of the political community, including its immigration control policies (Abizadeh 2008, p. 44).[8] Another way of looking at this dilemma is to notice that while the liberal state endeavours to eliminate borders dividing its own social classes or ethnic minorities, it takes for granted an external discrimination between citizens and non-citizens. This political tension, in turn, results in competing ethical claims (Gibney 1999, p. 173).[9] Thus, detention throws open the door on activities that may turn out to be too freedom -restricting within the larger rubric of a legitimate right to control borders.

Warehousing, containment and 'safety zones'

Detention is increasingly taking place outside the borders of the state that is orchestrating it. Asylum seekers who may have otherwise taken refuge in the Global North are arrested and/or forced to remain in the South while awaiting permission to travel onwards. If these people cannot make it to Europe or North America, they cannot technically claim asylum in those places. Writing in the European context, Juss (2005, pp. 766–767) argues that, faced with a growing population of asylum seekers arriving in the late-1990s and early-2000s, 'European Member States set upon a coordinated approach to systematically impose visa requirements on the nationals of most less developed, immigrant producing countries and underpinned these requirements with financial sanctions against carriers'. The cumulative effect has been an 'externalization' of migration controls to the periphery of Europe and beyond, and an overall reduction in asylum seekers' chances of reaching wealthier states that could provide them with long-term protection.

A key element in the European externalisation of asylum has been establishing centres for processing asylum applications outside the European Union's frontier (Lavenex and Uçarer 2004, Mainwaring 2012, p. 696). Likewise, the 2002 Pacific Solution was initiated by Australia to interdict boats carrying asylum seekers and reroute them for processing on the Pacific island of Nauru. People held in these detention centres are often denied the right to work, to unite with their families, to enjoy the freedoms of association, assembly and expression, and to own property (Van Hook 2009). In other words, instead of allocating more places, measures are being put in place to interdict and detain people in states neighbouring the places they fled, thereby keeping them far from the borders of the Global North where their asylum claims must be heard.

Ethical arguments in favor of externalised detention centres are not uncommon. For example, the border control defender David Miller offers cautious endorsement for such a proposal in his 2005 book chapter, 'Immigration: The case for limits'. In this well-known argument, Miller claims that the nation is the best sphere in which to achieve distributive justice. In his moderate interpretation of liberal nationalism, the rights of the national community are valued over and above individual claims for rights and universal equality. Miller provides arguments in favour of admissions control rooted in the significance to the community of culture, population control, and social trust and welfare. He is seeking a fair balance of costs and benefits imposed by immigration on both states and individuals.[10] On a state level, nations have a right to decide whether to restrict their numbers, live more ecologically and humanely, or do neither and bear the costs (Miller 2005, p. 202). In addition, the liberal state is morally obligated to provide sanctuary to asylum seekers and conduct migrant selection without bias or prejudice (Silverman 2013, pp. 161–163).

For Miller, the national community generates social goods over time, and it is only within the bounds of that particular community that the value of those goods can be fully appreciated and utilised (Miller 2005, pp. 197–198). Yet, he acknowledges the unfairness of people being consigned to lives of poverty due to their citizenship being vested in their countries of birth, an arbitrary circumstance over which they would have had no choice and could not have demonstrated consent. For these individuals, the more wealthy states must

> either ensure that the basic rights of such people are protected in the places where they live – by aid, by intervention, or some other means – or they must help them to move to other communities where their lives will be better. Simply shutting one's borders and doing nothing else is not a morally defensible option here. (Miller 2005, p. 198)

Miller recognises the ethical wrongfulness of 'doing nothing else' in relation to asylum seekers, and so he encourages resettlement abroad. But due to his aforementioned commitments to culture, population control, and social trust and welfare, Miller is keen to preserve individual states' discretion to decide how, when, and to whom asylum is granted (Miller 2005, p. 203). He therefore puts forward the innovative proposal of creating 'safety zones' close to the site of conflict and intervention to deal with the causes of the rights violations. Miller acknowledges the 'danger that the temporary solution becomes semi-permanent, and this is unacceptable because refugees are owed more than the immediate protection of their basic rights – they are owed something like the chance to make a proper life for themselves' (Miller 2005, p. 203).

Upon closer inspection, it seems that Miller is not attuned to the realities of migration, asylum, and containment on the ground, and may be providing tacit endorsement for detention as a 'resolution' for immigration and refugee issues. The migration studies literature explains that asylum crises by and large arise in regions of turmoil, and asylum seekers flee from one resource-poor state to another (Kritzman-Amir 2009, p. 361). Such events are typically marked by 'a suddenness, violence, and magnitude that can swiftly overwhelm the resources of a first-asylum state that is only linked to the flow by an accident of nature-its fortuitous proximity to the source country' (Schuck 1997, p. 273). Worldwide statistics support this depiction: around 'four-fifths of the world's asylum seekers flee to neighbouring states, reflected in the large refugee populations seen, for example, in Pakistan (1.7 million people), Iran (886,500), Kenya (566,500) and Chad (366,500)' (UNHCR: The UN Refugee Agency 2012).

The institutionalisation of detention centres abroad through funding and operating externalised processing centres and refugee camps is becoming increasingly permanent. This trend reflects a turn away from durable solutions – such as voluntary repatriation, permanent local integration in the country of first asylum, or resettlement – and towards detention. This practice of holding asylum seekers and irregular immigrants outside the borders of their destination states at the behest of those states is an integral step in the process referred to as 'containment' by Chimni (1998) and as 'warehousing' by the NGO and advocacy communities. It is interdiction, or arrest and detention, by another name.

On a normative level, Miller's safety zones are more promising. This proposal fulfils liberal states' immediate obligations to provide protection for people in imminent danger of persecution. Safety zones also allow states to gain knowledge of the potential future members of their community and to evaluate their suitability for permanent resettlement in their territories. However, they are undoubtedly problematic for a number of reasons. First and foremost, safety zones are, at bottom, glorified detention centres. They restrict asylum seekers and irregular immigrants to a certain place in the South for an unspecified period of time in order to suit the needs and convenience of the destination state in the North. In addition, safety zones appear to be a variation of the 'prison with three walls' argument: despite being ostensibly free to leave, safety zone inhabitants are actually forced to stay because of their unresolved immigration statuses. Without prior adjudication on their migrant or refugee status, the possibility of leaving the safety zone is largely illusory because continued, even indefinite, inhabitation is often more attractive than the prospect of returning to face the situation from which the individual was migrating away from initially (Silverman 2013, p. 173).

Conclusion: insights for normative theory from a study of detention

There are at least three additional insights for normative theory that can be gained from unmasking the roles played by detention in the immigration admissions debate. The first pertains to the temporal and spatial aspects of immigration enforcement; the second to the personification of the otherwise unknown figure of the 'refugee' or the 'immigrant'; and the third to the assuagement of liberals' concerns about the ethics of excluding people from entry into a state's territory.

First, normative theorists tend to adhere to an implicit assumption about the ways that decisions to admit or exclude are taken. Barriers of access are meant to coordinate to the physical boundaries of the state. Border guards are supposed to make quick decisions that swiftly lead to either deportation or leave to remain. Other than for the privileged traveller with favoured documents, however, these decisions often take place across time and in a variety of settings. Indeed, detention demonstrates the virtual impossibility of realising such a neat elision: in truth, immigration enforcement occurs at any point during someone's stay in another state, and it can be a drawn-out process inside and outside of a state's territorial borders. Admissions decisions are discretionary decisions taken by a variety of actors working under non-ideal constraints. The period of waiting for official admission can be drawn out for months and potentially years as an individual's case winds its way through the legal system. An increasing number of people are held in detention throughout this process, and the state must grapple with how to balance respect for due process rights against the daily deterioration of a detainee's well-being. The temporal aspect also extends past the initial admission or exclusion decision: detention leaves lifelong effects on the former detainee's psyche that curbs his or her senses of belonging to the community and trust in the government, two values that are essential for a functioning welfare state.

Second, the study of detention refocuses attention on the problems that can arise when scholars engaging in the immigration admissions debate depict migrants as faceless and nameless. Unless discussing, for instance, guest workers or denizens in a general sense, it is rare for normative theorists to delve into age, race, class, or other personal characteristics.[11] In this way, the immigration admissions system – including, presumably, the detention estate – can be presented as roundly fair and non-discriminatory so as to elide over the tensions mentioned above, amongst other aims. In practice, however, men and certain minorities are routinely singled out for discriminatory treatment, and this

119

prejudice is revealed when detention is brought into the equation. For example, in 2011, the majority of UK immigration detainees were single men from minority ethnic groups who had applied for asylum at some point during their immigration processes. The routine presence in detention of unaccompanied minors or families with children would probably be roundly condemned by *all* normative theorists, if they knew about this consequence of border control.

Third and most importantly, detention glosses over the virtually irreconcilable ethical conflicts intrinsic to the immigration admissions debate. An unqualified right to enter would entail a wholesale rethinking of state sovereignty and the migrant-citizen-state hierarchy. It would force states to wrestle with questions of historic injustice, blame, and restitution in determining who owes what to whom. In the meantime, detention allows states to hold non-citizens – and these weighty questions – at bay.

Overall, then, detention highlights the extreme physical consequences of the theoretical dilemmas of admission and exclusion. Importantly, the findings of this paper suggest that normative theorists cannot afford to diminish or relegate detention. David Miller's 'safety zones' proposal illustrates the challenges involved in confronting the roles that detention plays in immigration and asylum control strategies. While the idea of safety zones initially seems to meet the normative thresholds of an ethically satisfactory practice, closer inspection reveals it as a new variation on the old idea of detention for the convenience of destination states. Miller commits the sleight of hand common to border control defenders by renaming and repackaging detention into something more innocuous; more seriously, he does not grapple with the serious harms caused by exporting detention policies and practices abroad. The safety zones proposal provides further evidence of the dangers posed to normative theorists when they underestimate the ethical and practical consequences of detention being meted out to an increasingly large number of people around the world.

Acknowledgements

The author would like to thank Patti Lenard, Crispino Akakpo and the anonymous reviewer from CRISPP for their extremely useful comments and suggestions, as well as Bridget Anderson, Joseph H. Carens, Cathryn Costello, Matthew J. Gibney and Daniel J. Lowinsky for their insightful criticism on earlier versions of this argument. Any mistakes remain the author's own.

Notes

1. De Genova (2004, 2007) describes the constant vulnerability of irregular migrants and asylum seekers to deportation as 'deportability' and their vulnerability to detention as 'detainability'. He writes that 'selectively targeted indefinite and protracted detentions against an identifiable minority uphold and sustain racialized suspicion, and confirm that minority's more general susceptibility for detention – their *detainability*' (De Genova 2007, p. 434).

2. Of these 20 convictions, 6 were for sex offences – but not against children – 3 for violence, and 11 for actual bodily harm and grievous bodily harm.
3. Cornelisse (2010, p. 249) points out that the enjoyment of personal liberty is inscribed in Article 39 of the Magna Carta of 1215 and, thus, the English Habeas Corpus Acts of 1640 and 1679 codified an already existing procedure by which somebody deprived of his liberty could challenge detention by the King and Council.
4. Namely, *Amuur v. France* (1996) EHRR 533; *Chahal v. United Kingdom* (1997) 23 EHRR 413; and *R (Saadi) v Secretary of State for the Home Department* (2002) UKHL 41.
5. Crimmigration scholars examine the nexus of criminal justice, state administration, immigration law, civil and human rights, and security spheres, usually in a given national context. See e.g. Banks (2008), Hernández (2012), Stumpf (2006), and Welch (2012).
6. For Agamben, perhaps the most well-known critic of detention, the detention centre is a form of violence without juridical form that places its occupants in a condition of suspension outside the reach of law. This state of exception normalises and spatialises power while standing outside of power. For Agamben, the state of exception/detention centre practically defines modern political life (Agamben 1998, 2005). Cf. Edkins and Pin-Fat (2005), Silverman (2008), and Tyler (2006).
7. I develop further these four reasons that go some way towards explaining normative theorists' relative silence on immigration detention compared to other scholars in Silverman (2013).
8. See also Aleinikoff (2007, p. 424), Bosniak (2008, p. 9), and Carens (1992, p. 25). Cf. Joppke (2005) for an argument that the sway of an egalitarian, universalistic logic has diminished the potency of sovereignty and self-determination as the basis for exclusion of immigrants. Hence, Joppke is arguing that this fundamental tension that is central to normative discussion of immigrant exclusion is not as severe as one might think.
9. Normative theorists of immigration usually seek to resolve this tension by concluding that although borders and immigration regimes are illiberal in themselves, they serve as liberalism's enabling condition: as Ackerman (1980, p. 95) concludes, '[t]he only reason for restricting immigration is to protect the on-going process of liberal conversation itself'. Or, as Barry (1992, p. 283) puts it, there can be normatively valid reasons for immigration control.
10. 'I have tried to hold a balance between the interest that migrants have in entering the country they want to live in, and the interest that political communities [have] in determining their own character' (Miller 2005, p. 204).
11. In different contexts, Coole (2000), Kittay (2009), Mills (2000, 2009) and Pateman (1998) point out the dangers of normative theorists' selective blindness towards race, gender, and general minority views and positions.

References

Abizadeh, A., 2008. Democratic theory and border coercion: no right to unilaterally control your own borders. *Political theory*, 36, 37–65.

Ackerman, B.A., 1980. *Social justice in the liberal state*. New Haven, CT: Yale University Press.

Agamben, G., 1998. *Homo sacer: sovereign power and bare life*. Stanford, CA: Stanford University Press.

Agamben, G., 2005. *State of exception*. Chicago, IL: University of Chicago Press.

Aleinikoff, T.A., 2007. Comments on the rights of others. *European journal of political theory*, 6, 424–430.

Banks, J., 2008. The criminalisation of asylum seekers and asylum policy. *Prison service journal*, 175, 43–49.

Barry, B., 1992. The quest for consistency: a sceptical view. *In*: B. Barry and R.E. Goodin, eds. *Free movement: ethical issues in the transnational migration of people and of money*. New York: Harvester Wheatsheaf, 279–287.

BBC World Service, T., 2006. *How the deportation story emerged* [online]. Available from: http://news.bbc.co.uk/1/hi/uk_politics/4945922.stm [Accessed 16 October 2010].

Bhui, H.S., 2013. The changing approach to child detention and its implications for immigration detention in the UK. *Prison service journal*, 205 (Special edition: migration, nationality and detention), 23–28.

Bosniak, L., 2008. *The citizen and the alien: dilemmas of contemporary membership*. Oxford: Princeton University Press.

Bosworth, M., 2011. *Deportation, detention, and foreign national prisoners in England and Wales*. University of Oxford Legal Research Paper Series No. 33/2011. Oxford: University of Oxford, 30.

Carens, J.H., 1992. Migration and morality: a liberal egalitarian perspective. *In*: B. Barry and R.E. Goodin, eds. *Free movement: ethical issues in the transnational migration of people and of money*. London: Harvester Wheatsheaf, 25–47.

Chimni, B.S., 1998. The geopolitics of refugee studies: a view from the south. *Journal of refugee studies*, 11, 350–374.

Clayton, G., 2006. *Textbook on immigration and asylum law*. 2nd ed. Oxford: Oxford University Press.

Cornelisse, G., 2010. *Immigration detention and human rights: rethinking territorial sovereignty*. Leiden: Martinus Nijhoff Publishers.

Coole, D., 2000. Cartographic convulsions: public and private reconsidered. *Political theory*, 28, 337–354.

Costello, C., 2012. Human rights and the elusive universal subject: immigration detention under international human rights and EU law. *Indiana journal of global legal studies*, 19, 257–303.

Costello, C. and Kaytaz, E., 2013. *Building empirical research into alternatives to detention: perceptions of asylum-seekers and refugees in Toronto and Geneva* [online]. UNHCR: The UN Refugee Agency. Available from: http://www.unhcr.org/51c1c5cf9.html [Accessed 20 June 2013].

Crawley, H., 2011. *What are the alternatives to child detention?* COMPAS Breakfast Briefings. Oxford: ESRC Centre on Migration, Policy, and Society, 2.

Crépeau, F., 2012. A/HRC/20/24: report of the special rapporteur on the human rights of migrants, François Crépeau. *In*: *Human Rights Council twentieth session, agenda item 3: promotion and protection of all human rights, civil, political, economic, social and cultural rights, including the right to development*. Geneva: United Nations General Assembly, 20.

De Genova, N.P., 2004. The legal production of Mexican/migrant 'illegality'. *Latino studies*, 2, 160–185.

De Genova, N.P., 2007. The production of culprits: from deportability to detainability in the aftermath of 'homeland security'. *Citizenship studies*, 11, 421–448.

Díaz Jr., J., 2011. Immigration policy, criminalization and the growth of the immigration industrial complex: restriction, expulsion, and eradication of the undocumented in the US. *Western criminology review*, 12, 35–54.

Edkins, J. and Pin-Fat, V., 2005. Through the wire: relations of power and relations of violence. *Millennium – journal of international studies*, 34, 1–24.

Gammeltoft-Hansen, T. and Sørensen, N.N., eds., 2012. *The migration industry and the commercialization of international migration*. Abingdon: Routledge.

Gibney, M.J., 1999. Liberal democratic states and responsibilities to refugees. *The American political science review*, 93, 169–181.

Golash-Boza, T.M., 2009. The immigration industrial complex: why we enforce immigration policies destined to fail. *Sociology compass*, 3, 295–309.

Griffiths, M., 2010. *'I'm not a criminal but I've been here 11 months' – the criminalisation of asylum seekers in a British immigration detention centre* [online]. Centre on Migration, Policy, and Society. Available from: http://tinyurl.com/2uju4al [Accessed 10 October 2010].

Hailbronner, K., 2007. Detention of asylum seekers. *European journal of migration and law*, 9, 159–172.

Hernández, C.C.G., 2012. The perverse logic of immigration detention: unraveling the rationality of imprisoning immigrants based on markers of race and class otherness. *Columbia journal of race and law*, 1, 353–364.

Hirschl, R., 2000. 'Negative' rights vs. 'Positive' entitlements: a comparative study of judicial interpretations of rights in an emerging neo-liberal economic order. *Human Rights Quarterly*, 22 (4), 1060–1098.

Juss, S.S., 2005. The decline and decay of european refugee policy. *Oxford Journal of Legal Studies*, 25 (4), 749–792.

Jesuit Refugee Service – Europe, 2011. *From deprivation to liberty: alternatives to detention in Belgium, Germany and the United Kingdom*. Brussels: Jesuit Refugee Service – Europe, 58.

Joppke, C., 2005. Exclusion in the liberal state: the case of immigration and citizenship policy. *European journal of social theory*, 8 (1), 42–61.

Kessler, B., 2008–2009. In jail, no notice, no hearing … no problem – a closer look at immigration detention and the due process standards of the international covenant on civil and political rights. *American University international law review*, 24, 571–607.

Kittay, E.F., 2009. The ethics of philosophizing: ideal theory and the exclusion of people with severe cognitive disabilities. *In*: L. Tessman, ed. *Feminist ethics and social and political philosophy: theorizing the non-ideal*. London: Springer, 121–148.

Kritzman-Amir, T., 2009. Not in my backyard: on the morality of responsibility sharing in refugee law. *Brookings journal of international law*, 34, 355–394.

Laegaard, S., 2010. What is the right to exclude immigrants? *Res Publica*, 16, 245–262.

Lavenex, S. and Uçarer, E.M., 2004. The external dimension of Europeanization: the case of immigration policies. *Cooperation and conflict*, 39, 417–443.

Lorek, A., *et al.*, 2009. The mental and physical health difficulties of children held within a British immigration detention center: a pilot study. *Child abuse and neglect*, 33, 573–585.

Mainwaring, C., 2012. Constructing a crisis: the role of immigration detention in Malta. *Population, space and place*, 18, 687–700.

McGinley, A. and Trude, A., 2012. *Positive duty of care? The mental health crisis in immigration detention*. A briefing paper by the Mental Health in Immigration Detention Project. London: AVID (Association of Visitors to Immigration Detainees) & BID (Bail for Immigration Detainees), 20.

Miller, D., 2005. Immigration: the case for limits. *In*: A.I. Cohen and C.H. Wellman, eds. *Contemporary debates in applied ethics*. Oxford: Blackwell Publishing, 193–206.

Miller, D., 2012. Grounding human rights. *Critical review of international social and political philosophy*, 15, 407–427.

Mills, C.W., 2000. Race and the social contract tradition. *Social identities*, 6, 441–462.

Mills, C.W., 2009. Rawls on race/race in rawls. *The southern journal of philosophy*, 47 (S1), 161–184.

Oberman, K., 2009. *Immigration and freedom of movement*. Thesis (DPhil). Oxford: University of Oxford, 272.

Pateman, C., 1998. Myth, history, and democracy: Alien reflections. *Social Text*, 56, 5.

Physicians for Human Rights and The Bellevue/NYU Program for Survivors of Torture, 2003. *From persecution to prison: the health consequences of detention for asylum seekers*. Cambridge, MA: Physicians for Human Rights, 230.

Sampson, R., Mitchell, G., and Bowring, L., 2011. *There are alternatives: a handbook for preventing unnecessary immigration detention*. Melbourne: International Detention Coalition and the La Trobe Refugee Research Centre.

Schuck, P.H., 1997. Refugee burden-sharing: a modest proposal. *Yale journal of international law*, 22, 243–297.

Shachar, A., 2007. The shifting border of immigration regulation. *Stanford journal of civil rights and civil liberties*, 3, 165–195.

Silove, D., Steel, Z., and Watters, C., 2000. Policies of deterrence and the mental health of asylum seekers. *Journal of the American Medical Association*, 284, 604–611.

Silverman, S.J., 2008. Redrawing the lines of control: what political action undertaken by refugees in border detention centres tell us about international politics. *In*: *Proceedings of the dead/lines: contemporary issues in legal and politics theory conference*. Edinburgh: University of Edinburgh.

Silverman, S.J., 2011. *Policy briefing: immigration detention in the UK* [online]. COMPAS. Available from: http://www.migrationobservatory.ox.ac.uk/briefings/immigration-detention-uk [Accessed 20 June 2011].

Silverman, S.J., 2013. *The normative ethics of immigration detention in liberal states*. Thesis (DPhil). Oxford: University of Oxford, 256.

Steel, Z., *et al.*, 2006. Impact of immigration detention and temporary protection on the mental health of refugees. *The British journal of psychiatry*, 188, 58–64.

Stone, C., 2000. Supervised release as an alternative to detention in removal proceedings: some promising results of a demonstration project. *Georgetown immigration law journal*, 14, 673–688.

Stumpf, J., 2006. The crimmigration crisis: immigrants, crime, and sovereign power. *American University law review*, 56, 367–419.

Transactional Records Access Clearinghouse (TRAC), 2013. *Legal noncitizens receive longest ICE detention* [online]. Available from: http://trac.syr.edu/whatsnew/email.130603.html [Accessed 15 July 2013].

Trujillo-Pagan, N., 2013. Emphasizing the 'complex' in the 'immigration industrial complex'. *Critical sociology*, 40 (1), 29–46.

Tyler, I., 2006. 'Welcome to Britain': the cultural politics of asylum. *European journal of cultural studies*, 9, 185–202.

UK Home Office, T., 1998. *Fairer, faster and firmer – a modern approach to immigration and asylum* [online]. The UK Home Office. Available from: http://www.archive.official-documents.co.uk/document/cm40/4018/4018.htm [Accessed 1 July 2010].

UNHCR: The UN Refugee Agency, 2012. *Global trends report: 800,000 new refugees in 2011, highest this century* [online]. Available from: http://www.unhcr.org/4fd9e6266.html [Accessed 12 April 2012].

Van Hook, I., 2009. *Policy option: warehousing* [online]. Policy Options. Available from: http://policyoptions.pbworks.com/w/page/17513339/Policy%20Option%3A%20Warehousing [Accessed 10 July 2013].

Welch, M., 2012. The sonics of crimmigration in Australia: wall of noise and quiet manoeuvring. *British journal of criminology*, 52, 324–344.

Wilcox, S., 2009. The open borders debate on immigration. *Philosophy Compass*, 4 (5), 813–821.

Wilsher, D., 2008. The administrative detention of non-nationals pursuant to immigration control: international and constitutional law perspectives. *International and comparative law quarterly*, 53, 897–934.

Young, A., 1991. All along the watchtower: arbitrary detention and the police function. *Osgoode Hall law journal*, 29, 329–398.

Climate change refugees

Matthew Lister

Law Clerk to Judge Dolores Sloviter, U.S. Court of Appeals for the 3rd Circuit, Philadelphia, PA, USA

Under the UNHCR definition of a refugee, set out in the 1967 Protocol Relating to the Status of Refugees, people fleeing their homes because of natural disasters or other environmental problems do not qualify for refugee status and the protection that come from such status. In a recent paper, I defended the essentials of the UNHCR definition on the grounds that refugee status and protection is best reserved for people who can only be helped by granting them refuge in a safe state for an indefinite period of time, and argued that this does not include most people fleeing from natural disasters. This claim is most strongly challenged by the possibility of displacement from climate change. In this paper, I will explore to what degree the logic of the refugee convention, as set out in my earlier paper, can and should be extended to those fleeing the results of climate change.

Introduction

The idea of a 'climate change refugee' is a comparatively new one. Despite the fact that international migration in response to environmental factors has been both normal and common throughout human history, the first significant discussions of movement based primarily on climate change-related factors[1] started only in the 1990's, and at this time, the discussion was mostly undertaken by scientists interested in climate change, not by those doing legal, practical, or normative work on refugees and forced migration[2] (McAdam 2012, pp. 1–3). The highly comprehensive three-volume set, *Immigration and Asylum from 1900 to the Present* (Gibney and Hansen, 2005) does not discuss climate change specifically at all, nor does it have entries for island states such as Tuvalu or Kiribati, often thought to be among the most likely to produce climate change refugees.[3] A recent volume on forced migration, (Crepeau *et al.*, 2006) covering many different problems and perspectives, included no coverage of climate change. While a large legal and practical (or, perhaps, intended to be practical) literature has developed over the last several years,[4] more normatively focused work has been relatively sparse. Two of the most important recent normative works on refugees and asylum, Gibney (2005) and Price (2009), for example, give no significant discussion to the topic of climate change at all.[5] While in the last few years, there have been a small number of philosophical papers addressing, at least in some sense, the problem of climate change refugees, (Risse 2009, Nine 2010, Kolers 2012) I shall register some significant worries about the treatment of the problem presented there.

In this paper, I will provide a normative foundation for the idea of a climate change refugee, and show how this category can be made to fit within the logic (though not the current legal language) of the UN Refugee convention. In doing so, I will draw on my earlier work on refugees (Lister 2013) showing how the normative basis for refugee protection I developed there can be extended to include the most relevant groups affected by climate change. While this is not, by any means, a general solution to the problems faced by people threatened by climate change, I will argue that crafting such protection has an important role to play in a scheme of responses.

This approach, if successful, has several advantages over its rivals. Though it would require modifying or adding to the current terms of the UN refugee convention, it would not require a fundamental shift in the underlying logic that I have described. If this is so, we would not need a new 'territorial approach',[6] nor need we make reference to ideas like the 'common ownership of the earth'.[7] And, we would not need to fundamentally recast refugee protection in terms of a 'human rights' approach,[8] one that depends, it seems to me, on greatly modifying and expending our understanding of human rights and how they function in international law. Although I would contend that the more modest change I suggest is the correct one in any evaluation, the more important argument for it in this setting is its greater degree of 'progressive conservatism'.[9] This is a central concern in that, in cases like those at issue in this paper and on topics such as refugees in general, feasibility and likelihood of successful adoption of a proposed change are fundamental, and of crucial importance. What we want is a system that will do the most justice to people given plausibly achievable goals, starting from the situation we find ourselves in. Proposing views that would require major changes to our normative systems, as those discussed above would, will often lead to inaction, inertia, and greater injustice. In cases such as this, the practicality of a proposal is not a mere detail, but a fundamental concern. More 'ideal' proposals are often worse than useless – they may lead to greater injustice. Thus, I will show how my extension of the logic of the UN Refugee Convention fares better than other proposals in terms of being a useful step to help those in need. Furthermore, even as a matter of theory, if we can make do with a more conservative account, this is to be preferred to an approach that requires us to accept controversial accounts of territory or common ownership of the earth. If we can achieve acceptable results with less controversial premises, both widespread agreement and correctness are more likely to result.

The 'logic' of the UN refugee convention and the case of climate refugees

The 1967 Protocol[10] to the UN Convention on the Status of Refugees defines a refugee as one who:

> Owing to a well-founded fear of being persecuted for reasons of race, religion, nationality, membership in a particular social group, or political opinion, is out-side the country of his nationality and is unable or, owing to such fear, is unwilling to avail himself of the protection of that country; or who, not having a nationality and being outside the country of his former habitual residence, is unable or, owing to such fear, is unwilling to return to it.

This definition does not, in any plausible way, cover people fleeing their homes because of environmental disruption, including disruption caused by climate change.[11] Those fleeing disruption caused by climate change are not plausibly thought of as being persecuted, and so cannot have a well-founded fear of persecution. Generally speaking, the danger caused by climate change is indiscriminate, and hence the danger faced is not 'on account of' one of the 'protected grounds'– race, religion, nationality, membership in a particular social group, or political opinion.[12] Given this, two essential elements of the refugee definition are missing in the case of those fleeing the impact of climate change.

However, I have recently argued (Lister 2013) that the best way to understand the logic of the Refugee Convention – the normative force behind it – is to ask what, if anything, makes refugees a normatively distinct group from others who need aid from the international community.[13] In this earlier work, I argued that the best way to understand what is morally distinct about refugees is to ask to whom what we owe to refugees is owed. In that work, I assumed the fairly standard idea that what is owed to refugees is, first, *non-refoulemont* – the obligation to not return those fleeing danger of the appropriate sort to a state where they would face this danger – and, at least eventually, a 'durable solution'– the right to remain in a safe country indefinitely, with eventual access to full membership. In that work, I argued that the group picked out by the Refugee Convention definition was normatively distinct from others needing help from the international community, because such people could only, or at least could best, be helped by providing them the particular remedy of asylum, understood as including both *non-refoulemont* and a 'durable solution.'[14] To the extent that those picked out by the Convention definition had this trait, and other groups needing aid did not, it made sense to treat Convention refugees as a morally distinct group. This, I argued, was the logic of the Refugee Convention.

There was, however, a lacuna in this earlier argument. There I maintained that if other groups not picked out by the Refugee Convention definition also could only be helped by granting them asylum (as defined above), then the logic of the Refugee Convention, even if not its terms as currently accepted, would tell in favor of extending refugee status and protection to these others in need of aid as well. I provided some argument as to why I did not think this would be a common case, but held open the possibility that certain environmental displacements, including (but not necessarily limited to) climate change, might fit this standard (Lister 2013). It is my goal in this section of the paper to fill the gap in my earlier argument by showing how the logic of the Refugee Convention can apply, without significant modification, to certain people displaced by climate change-related environmental problems.[15] I shall argue that refugee status, and with it the right to *non-refoulemont* and a durable solution, is owed to the subset of those displaced by climate change or other environmental disruptions of expected indefinite duration, where international movement is necessitated, and where the threat is not just to a favored or traditional way of life, but to the possibility of a decent life at all.

In the next section, I shall explain why refugee status and the right to asylum ought to be extended to the group picked out above, but need not be extended to others displaced or facing displacement from climate change. The number of people who face serious difficulty from climate change is very large in comparison to the number who would be picked out by this account, so it is important to see why only this group must be given this particular form of aid. But, before showing that, it is necessary to reiterate two points. First, there will often be a moral obligation owed by the international community or by individual states to people harmed by climate change other than that I discuss here. That a person or group is not properly thought of as a refugee does not mean that they are not in need of, or owed, other forms of aid. Secondly, and relatedly, this is only one small part of what may be owed to those harmed by climate change. It would be foolish to think that extending refugee protection, or even granting other forms of migration rights, could solve all of the problems that are likely to arise. So, this approach will not solve all or even most problems. But, it is, I shall argue, and important piece of the proper international response to climate change, and so worth working out in some detail. As I have argued before, making our duties clear is one important step to fulfilling them (Lister 2013).

Why these limits?

Each of the limits I argue for here has some degree of parallel with the logic of the Refugee Convention, as I have elsewhere described it. Understanding these limits, and why they are relevant to granting refugee protection, is our next step. First, however, it is worth reiterating that asylum is a particularly weighty remedy, one requiring a state to take steps it otherwise would have no obligation to take, and therefore may only be required when it is the only, or perhaps clearly the best, remedy for a situation. This is perhaps especially important for explaining why asylum is the proper remedy for environmental problems expected to be of indefinite duration, but not for those expected to cause only temporary displacement.

If an environmental problem is of temporary duration, such as the typical damage from a hurricane, earthquake, or flood, it is reasonable to expect people to return to their homes once the danger has passed, at least if help in restoring communities to functioning levels is granted.[16] Because of this, some form of temporary protection will usually suffice for those forced from their homes because of environmental problems.[17] In earlier work, I noted how the situation is different for those who face persecution on the basis of a protected ground. Because this threat comes from a state (or a non-state group the state cannot or will not control) we must assume that the threat is of indefinite extension.[18] This is part of what makes asylum, including a durable solution, appropriate in such cases. While this typically does not apply to those fleeing natural disasters, it may plausibly apply in the case of certain sorts of environmentally based displacements. The most plausible cases involve low-lying islands faced with rising sea levels and, perhaps even more importantly, rapidly decreasing access to freshwater.[19] In cases such as these, the threat that leads people to abandon their homes is unlikely to be short term. For such people, temporary protection will not suffice. In certain cases, those discussed below, the need for a permanent solution to the problem will justify asylum as a remedy.

The next issue is the role of *international* or cross-border movement in the analysis. Although supposedly 'sinking islands' have caught much of the public (and philosophical) attention, as Jane McAdam (2012, p. 16) notes, the large majority of migration related to climate change will be, or could be, internal.[20] This is unsurprising, given that climate change has, and will have, effects all over the globe, but only a small percentage of the currently inhabited planet will become uninhabitable. (Or so we may hope. If this is not so, we have more significant problems than any theory of migration can help us with.) Even in the case of countries facing quite serious environmental problems plausibly tied to climate change, such as Bangladesh, the vast majority of the projected movement will be internal to the country (McAdam 2012, pp. 166–172).

That the majority of migration plausibly tied to climate change is likely to be internal is relevant for two reasons. First, it throws serious doubts on 'alarmist' views of the likely migratory impact of climate change. As McAdam (2012, pp. 4–5) notes, projections of millions of people crossing international borders are both not based on sound estimates and empirical study, and threaten to create the sort of panic and backlash against those actually displaced across international borders that has tended to leave them unprotected.[21] Second, if people are able to relocate safely within their own country, there is no, or at least significantly less, reason to provide protection in another country. Aid may be given in-country.[22] In many cases, this will be preferable, not just to countries other than the one in need of aid, but also to those harmed, who may have no desire to leave their own countries, cultures, languages, friends, and so on. In such cases, there may even be an obligation to help the people remain within their own state rather than offering the option of coming to a new state, though, as with many issues in relation to international assistance, context will be important.[23]

In other cases, internal relocation will not be a plausible option. This may be so for all or for only a part of the population. (It may be, for example, that a low-lying island can support a very small population, but that the majority of its inhabitants will have to leave.) In such cases, we again are faced with a group of people who can only be helped by granting them residence in a safe, new, state, given our previous assumption that the condition in question is likely to be of indefinite duration. We see here, again, how some portion of those forced to move fit within the logic of the Refugee Convention definition. (In the sort of cases under consideration here, we also need not worry to the same degree that the 'country of origin' will oppose attempts at aid, a feature that I have elsewhere (Lister 2013) argued is of significant importance in determining the nature and scope of our duties. Noticing this helps us see how the logic of the refugee convention applies in both the case under consideration and in the more 'traditional' case.)

The final condition I defend, that the threat faced must be to the possibility of living a decent life at all, not merely to a favored or traditional way of life, is in part a corollary to the previous condition. Many people around the world face significant challenges to their favored or traditional ways of life due to environmental challenges tied to climate change. Farmers in the Mid-West of the United States, for example, have faced several years of significant drought thought by many to be influenced by climate change (Plumer 2012). If the already serious drought continues or worsens, it is plausible that these farmers will have to leave their homes and favored ways of life. Imagine, however, that one effect of climate change is that areas of the Canadian prairie not currently suitable for heavy agricultural work became capable of supporting the former way of life of displaced Mid-Western US farmers. Or consider a somewhat less hypothetical case. Many Yup'ik Eskimos in Alaska now face very significant challenges to their traditional way of life due to quickly decreasing ice coverage, melting permafrost, and related erosion (National Public Radio 2013). Imagine that the Yup'ik could continue their traditional way of life in nearby Siberia. In either of these cases, would there be an obligation for the country where the favored way of life could be continued – Canada or Russia – to grant entry to those displaced from their homes? I will argue that there is no such obligation.

There are several plausible bases for a duty to grant asylum to those facing the appropriate dangers (whatever they may be), but it does not seem that any of these would require granting admission to people merely because they face difficulties, even severe difficulties, in continuing a favored or traditional way of life. In earlier work (Lister 2013), I argued that either something like Rawls's 'duty of assistance' (Rawls 1999, pp. 105–113) or a 'duty of humanitarianism' (Gibney 2004, pp. 229–249) could ground such a duty. Perhaps other accounts, such as Risse's (2009) supposed 'common ownership of the earth' could also suffice. That many bases are available for this duty is one of its strengths – it need not depend on any one particular controversial theory, but is supported by several accounts. But on none of these accounts is what is owed the ability to continue any particular favored or traditional way of life.

We can see why this would be so when we consider the domestic case. Even in the domestic case, where duties to members are arguably significantly higher, there is no obligation to insure that all people must be able to continue or enjoy any particular way of life, so long as all people have a range of good lives open to them. In any society, it may be that unproblematic developments tend to render particular ways of life difficult or impossible. Changing tastes may render a form of life unviable, or democratically decided upon decisions about environmental stewardship may make certain lifestyles, such as logging, no longer available. Similarly, traditional religions may find it difficult or impossible to flourish or even survive in open societies where membership may not be enforced by law. But, in all of these cases, there is no obligation for the state to ensure that any particular way of life is able to flourish or survive.[24] As Rawls (1996, p. 197) states, 'there is no social world without loss: that is, no social world that does not exclude some ways of life that realize in special ways certain fundamental values.'

If domestic societies do not have an obligation to preserve or make possible all of the favored or traditional ways of life desired by their own citizens, it is hard to see how the international community could have such an obligation. But, if there is no such international obligation, then the fact that climate change made a traditional or favored way of life impossible within a certain territory would not imply a right to enter into a distinct state where the way in life in question could be pursued, unless this was as a matter of mutual agreement.[25] The case is different, however, if and when climate change or other forms of environmental difficulty makes any decent form of life at all impossible in a territory. Here, those threatened are not required merely to accept a different, less desired, form of life, but face the possibility of being unable to live a decent life at all. Such would be the case if climate change caused an island to have too little fresh water to support the population, for example. Assuming such danger to be country-wide,[26] those at risk would have no choice but to enter another country if they are to live any sort of decent life at all. I shall argue below that states receiving people fleeing from climate change or other environmental harms need not take steps to allow the victims to recreate their former styles of life beyond what is required by human rights, liberal principles of justice, and other such considerations, but here we can see clearly the difference between the two groups discussed in this section.

I have argued that the logic of the refugee convention can be plausibly extended to cover certain people fleeing from environmental harms, including climate change-related harms. This group is made up of people who are fleeing dangers expected to be of indefinite duration, who have no choice but to cross an international frontier, and where the risk is not just to a favored or traditional way of life, but to the ability to live a decent life at all.[27] This is a minority of people whose lives will be seriously impacted by climate change. But, I have tried to show, it is the subsection of those affected by climate change who are properly thought of as refugees, and so who ought to be eligible for asylum. While we should not underestimate the difficulties faced in changing the Refugee Convention to include this group, the reasons for doing so are, I hope, clear.

Is 'individualized' protection sufficient?

Asylum and refugee protection is 'individualistic' in several senses. First, even though group membership often figures into the justification for a claim to refugee protection, it is the individual in question, and not the group, who is typically thought to be owed protection. Additionally, refugee status determinations are typically made in an individualized way, rather than being applied to a group of people as a whole.[28] In this section of the paper, I will address these issues, focusing first on the more 'practical' issue of status determination, before returning to the more 'conceptual' issue of whether providing relief to individuals, as individuals, suffices to meet our moral duties.

McAdam (2012, p. 188) has noted that one potential problem in applying the Convention Refugee paradigm to those fleeing the effects of climate change is that the type of individualized status determinations that are typical of Convention refugees seem implausible and impractical in the case of mass flight. In assessing the extent to which individualized determinations are proper at all, we should distinguish between two scenarios. In the first case, an entire territory or state is rendered uninhabitable, requiring flight by all inhabitants. In the second, adverse environmental developments do not render the territory completely uninhabitable, but do make it so that only a much smaller fraction of the population may safely remain within the territory. In the first scenario, only minimally individualized determinations seem necessary. In such a case, determining that the person seeking protection is in fact from the state affected should be sufficient. State-wide application of protection with only minimal individualized determinations is used in several countries in relation to various sorts of temporary protected status.[29] I can see no obvious reason why, in the first scenario, more than this sort of minimal determination would be needed.

The second scenario is somewhat more complicated because, per hypothesis, not everyone from the threatened territory must leave, though most will have to. Here, a 'blanket' determination of the sort considered above may be less applicable. In such cases, the most plausible approach might be pre-departure screening of a minimal sort, establishing citizenship and identity, for example, and determination, in cooperation with the government of the territory, of those who will leave.[30] This would allow orderly processing with only minimally individualized determinations – deciding that people were who they said they were, and so on. Given the possibility of these procedures, worries about individualized processing in these cases do not seem to me to be decisive or perhaps even especially significant.

The deeper and perhaps more interesting question is the more conceptual one, of whether individualized remedies can satisfy our moral duties here.[31] Though there are significant differences between their views, both Cara Nine and Avery Kolers have argued that 'individualistic' remedies cannot meet our moral duties to those forced to flee their homes in the face of climate change,[32] and that 'corporate' remedies are instead needed. Many 'corporate' approaches favor 'territorial' remedies, seeking to remedy the harm suffered by those fleeing from climate change by transferring territory from existing states to those whose state can no longer support them.[33]

Both Nine and Kolers argue that 'individualistic' remedies, such as that applied by traditional refugee protection of the sort I have argued for, cannot suffice to remedy the wrong suffered by those who are displaced. The wrong in issue, according to corporate approaches, is that those displaced have been deprived of their 'collective right to self-determination,' (Nine 2010, p. 359) and face losing their 'political identity, political community, currency, civil society institutions, and perhaps even language' (Kolers 2012, p. 334). These harms, it is claimed, can only be compensated by granting a new territory to those who have fled their own. This is not just a right to enter a safe country, but the right to govern some new territory, on terms largely similar to how the group governed its own former territory. Importantly, this would be a right held by the group, and not by any particular member in it. In what follows, I shall argue that each part of this claim is mistaken. First, I shall argue that the international society does not owe the sort of right to self-determination to the displaced group suggested by the corporate approach. Rather, what is owed is the opportunity for each individual to be part of a self-determining group. Next, I will show that corporate accounts, but especially Kolers,' depend on an implausible account of responsibility for whatever plausibility they have. Finally, I will note that pragmatic concerns tell heavily in favor of individualistic approaches. Given that, in areas such as this, the feasibility of a theory is an essential feature, this is not a minor concern. If I am correct in these claims, then there will be significant reason to favor individualized over corporate responses in the type of cases we are considering.[34]

Corporate accounts such as Nine's and Kolers' depend on the notion that there is a right to self-determination, held by groups, that ought to be enforceable against the international community. Typically, this right would be operational within an existing territory, but, when a territory becomes unable to support the group in question, the right to self-determination entails at least a defeasible right to claim a new territory (Nine 2010, p. 366, Kolers 2012, p. 336). This claim is, at least, highly controversial. The sort of right to self-determination that it depends on is not recognized in international law, nor is it likely to be at any point soon. Of course, this does not settle the conceptual or moral issue, but does show that the account faces considerable problems with implementation. Perhaps more fundamentally, it is a controversial account of what self-determination requires even among those who recognize such a right for groups.

To see the controversial nature of the corporate view, we may note that, even among those who accept 'primary rights' accounts to self-determination and secession,[35] the view here would be an extreme one, in that it calls for not just the reorganization of an existing state among its current inhabitants, but the transfer of territory from one group to another, completely alien group.[36] This might suggest retreating to a less controversial 'remedial rights only' account for acquiring new territory, but such an account, if it were to be successful, would require attributions of responsibility that are not, for reasons I will discuss below, plausible. Finally, it is important to note that this approach is most likely to promote backlash against those in need of aid. If states believe that what is required of them, to help climate change refugees, is to give up significant portions of their territory, then aid is very unlikely to be forthcoming. This history of backlash against refugees in general, and the particular backlash against territorial claims in the case of Nauru, (McAdam 2012, pp. 147–153) strongly point in this direction, giving further reason to think that the territorial, 'corporate' approach is unworkable.[37]

What is plausibly owed to those displaced by climate change is a right, held by individuals, to be able to be full members in a polity that respects them and allows them sufficient autonomy. In the case of existing states with minimally just governments, this right is satisfied by not interfering with the legitimate government. But, it is a non-sequitur to suppose that this means, in the case of a destroyed state, that the old government should be given new territory. Rather, the relevant sort of self-determination can be fully supplied within the individual protection approach, as each individual would be provided the same sort of self-determination rights that anyone anywhere has – the right to take part in a just society. This would require respecting minority rights and protecting the rights of the displaced individuals, protection of language rights, and so on.[38] But, this may all be done without granting new territory to governments of no longer inhabitable states. Self-determination, properly understood, does not, then, tell against individualistic approaches.

Kolers has suggested another argument the might tell in favor of the corporate/territorial approach, one based on the supposed wrongdoing of industrialized states from which territory would be taken. Here, the wrongdoing of some states might call for compensation for those harmed in the form of a grant of new territory. If this were so, then a less controversial 'remedial rights' approach to self-determination might support corporate remedies for those displaced by climate change. We might think of this wrongdoing on analogy with either crime or tort, but neither approach supports a corporate/territorial view, I shall show.

Consider first the crime approach (Kolers 2012, p. 334). Criminal responsibility typically requires an intentional act that was prohibited at the time of its doing, and usually also requires that the bad results be foreseeable. This is an implausible description of the large majority of actions leading to climate change. As noted by Risse (2009, p. 282), emissions of green-house gases were completely legal at the time the majority of damage was done (and largely still is).[39] Furthermore, for most of the time when significant greenhouse gases were emitted, there was no wide-spread understanding of the danger. Perhaps an argument could be made about further release of gases, but it would be hard to show that these were proximate causes of the harms to those facing danger, as opposed to releases of gases in the past. If we want an analogy with crime to work, it is important to make sure there is a real analogy. At best, Kolers has not shown this, and the proposed analogy seems quite weak on several grounds.

Next consider the analogy with tort. Here, the basis for moral responsibility need not be as direct as with crime. There need not be a pre-exiting prohibition on the action causing the danger, for example. There may still be problems about foreseeability, but that is not my main worry. Rather, the most fundamental problem with the tort approach is that it depends on a highly controversial and, to my mind, implausible version of joint and several liability. Even the worst contributor to global warming will have only contributed a minority portion of the total amount of greenhouse gases. Yet, Kolers' corporate/territorial solution is one that can only be imposed on a particular state, putting the full burden on one country.[40] Such an approach is implausible on its face (especially when we note that actions by the threatened states are themselves significant contributors to their current situation; see McAdam (2012, pp. 123–127) but also has the negative result of making burden-sharing more difficult. The individualized approach, on the other hand, provides a straight-forward way to distribute shares of blame and so to partition burdens. Neither 'wrongdoing' argument, then, tells in favor of a corporate/territorial approach.

Finally, it is worth noting that neither Nine nor Kolers give any serious discussion to the situation of the current inhabitants of the territory to be re-distributed. Ignoring the impact on those who dissent to territorial transfers is a common problem in discussions of self-determination. That there is a problem is not even noted in the accounts under consideration.[41] But, without at least a gesture at this problem, we have no reason to think such an account can be successfully implemented without itself inflicting significant injustice.

Conclusion

Climate change is a complex and fiendishly difficult problem. No one approach is likely to do more than make a partial contribution to the necessary changes that it engenders. In this paper, I have argued that one part of an acceptable response is to see how refugee law might be extended to help some of those at risk, and have argued that these changes follow from the logic of the UN Refugee Convention. While, at best, this is only a small part of a complex puzzle, it may yet be an important one.

Acknowledgments

My thanks to Patti Tamara Lenard, Crispino Akakpo, Adam Hosein, Jaya Ramji-Nogales, and an anonymous referee for this journal for helpful comments and discussion. Nothing in this paper reflects an official position of the 3rd Circuit Court of Appeals or the US government.

Notes

1. We should note that climate change is almost always only one factor necessitating movement of peoples in the sort of case we are interested. There are no actual clear 'clean' cases. This, arguably, has some significant implications for some theories of duties to those who must flee their homes, implications ignored in some of the more purely philosophical discussions of the matter.
2. McAdam (2012, p. 3) notes that the term 'environmental refugee' was first used in a formal document in 1985, by Essam El-Hinnawi, but the term covers many more people than plausibly fall under the 'climate change refugee' category, and does not, for plausible reasons, give that category any special attention.
3. The work does include a discussion of migration from Bangladesh, another state often associated with climate change refugees, but this discussion focuses almost exclusively on politically related factors in relation with India (Abrar 2005).
4. This literature is very ably discussed in McAdam (2012). I am greatly indebted to it for my knowledge of this literature, and think that McAdam's book is clearly essential reading for anyone interested in this general subject. Howard Chang has also provided important consideration of the issue from the perspective of economic analysis. See Chang (2010). I briefly touch on some of Chang's points below, but do not have the space to consider all of his arguments in depth.
5. Price briefly discusses people fleeing from natural or environmental events that would prevent them from returning home within any fairly short time period, but does not mention climate change as a likely cause. See Price (2009, pp. 174–6).
6. Such an approach is advocated, in somewhat different ways, by both Nine (2010) and Kolers (2012). I shall show what is especially problematic about these approaches later in the paper.
7. As is advocated by Risse (2009).
8. As is, at least sometimes, advocated by McAdam (2012), among others. See also Karen Musalo (1994).
9. This term is due to Allen Buchanan, and suggests that a theory, 'should build upon, or at least not squarely contradict, the morally acceptable principles of the existing international legal system.' See Buchanan (2004, p. 63).
10. 1967 Protocol relating to the Status of Refugees, Article I section 2, incorporating by reference with modifications article 1 A(2) of the 1951 Convention on the Status of Refugees
11. See McAdams (2012, pp. 42–48) for a very helpful discussion of problems in trying to apply both the UN Refugee Convention, as well as various regional refugee conventions, in their current form, to the case of those fleeing climate change.

12. Of course, it is not unusual for people fleeing 'natural' disasters to be unequally subjected to danger *because of* one of the protected grounds. In such case, the people in question are subject to persecution and meet the 'nexus' requirement of the refugee definition, and hence are plausibly convention refugees. Such 'hybrid' cases contain an important element of human agency that is lacking in the 'clean' climate change refugee case. I discuss hybrid cases, and why they should be seen to fall under a fairly traditional reading of the refugee definition, in my paper, (Lister 2013).

13. People who cannot meet their basic needs on their own, but who can be adequately helped by their own governments, form another morally distinct category. These distinctions will be relevant further along in this paper.

14. Here, one of the differences between my approach and that set out by Matthew Price becomes clearer. I hold that the remedy of asylum is appropriate when this is the only or best way to help those in need. While I have argued that this typically follows the classical UN Refugee Convention, this connection is shallow rather than deep – on my account, there is no *special* connection with persecution on the basis of a protected ground, or with harm from a state government. Rather, it is simply the case that this sort of harm can typically only be remedied by granting asylum, while other types of harm may be addressed in other ways. My account, then, does not postulate a special relationship between asylum and political harm, nor with desire to provide a political rebuke to offending states, as does Price's. Though we sometimes argue for similar substantive conclusions, the logic of the arguments is quite different. This comes out in the case addressed by this paper, where the harm faced is not directly political. See Price (2009, pp. 24–94).

15. This extension need not be restricted to environmental displacement cause in part by climate change. The displacement of the inhabitants of Montserrat due to volcanic activity is a clear example.

16. As McAdam (2012, pp. 161–85) documents in her fieldwork in Bangladesh, those displaced by temporary environmental problems often have strong personal preferences to return to their homes as well. Given these preferences, a remedy that helps make this possible and likely is especially appropriate.

17. Most current forms of temporary protection have significant shortcomings, but this need not change the fundamental point. Furthermore, supposedly temporary protection often leads to long-term displacement, after which significant ties to the protective community are formed. This may lead to distinct grounds for allowing some people granted temporary protection to adjust to permanent resident status. For useful discussion on both of these points, see Price (2009, pp. 174–80). Adam Hosein, in an unpublished paper, 'The Fundamental Argument for Legalization', presents a particularly powerful and original argument for this claim (Hosein [unpublished]).

18. Of course, a state that engaged in persecution may be toppled or otherwise change. If this happens in a relatively short time period after the would-be refugee seeks protection, a 'changed circumstances' clause, such as that found in the asylum law of the US and other countries, may properly be invoked. For discussion of the 'cessation clause' in the refugee convention, see Guy Goodwin-Gill, (1998, pp.80–9). However, it is usually implausible to assume this will happen, and after a certain amount of time, a refugee would have built up a plausible claim to remain in the host country. For discussion on this last point, see Adam Hosein (unpublished).

19. For very helpful discussion of the actual likely mechanisms that could make island states such as Tuvalu or Kiribati uninhabitable, see McAdam (2012, pp. 123–127), and the work cited therein. It is worth noting that, while climate change is a likely

example of environmental or 'natural' problems that might render a territory indefinitely uninhabitable, the fit is far from perfect or exclusive. On the other hand, as will be discussed below, much of the damage caused by climate change will not render entire territories uninhabitable, indicating that not all climate change related movement must be addressed via the refugee approach.

20. Of course, if current immigration rules were changed, at least some movement that would, under current rules, be internal would likely rather be cross-border. But, for our purposes, what is most relevant is that much of the movement likely to be induced by climate change *could be* internal – crossing an international border is not, strictly speaking, necessary to avoid the most immediate and pressing dangers.

21. For helpful discussion of backlash against (often relatively small) movements of refugees, where large flows were feared, see Gibney, (2004, pp. 94–103, 177–192).

22. Howard Chang has argued that there are significant economic reasons to favor international migration in cases such as those I consider in this section. See Chang (2010, pp. 346–355). These are significant arguments in need of more consideration than I can give them here, but for now I shall merely note that they are largely pragmatic arguments, while I am here primarily interested in questions of moral obligation. States may, of course, decide that the best way for them to meet their duties to those who suffer from climate change is to allow more migration generally, but, if I am right, this is not a necessary conclusion from a moral perspective.

23. For example, if internal migration on a large scale would threaten to throw a whole country or significant part of it into chaos, while international migration would avoid this, then of course international migration would be preferable.

24. States plausibly have an obligation to help their own citizens whose ways of life have become unviable to transition to new ways of life. This might apply to midwest farmers or to the Yup'ik. It seems much less plausible to me that this duty is owed to citizens of other states.

25. We might think that considerations of causation and rightful compensation lead to greater duties here. This argument has some force, but is not, I think, fully convincing in the end. I address this issue further below.

26. Or, perhaps, nearly so. It might be that part of a country is subject to significant damage, while another part remains inhabitable, but the remaining part is not sufficient to support the entire population. This is, in fact, a fairly plausible scenario for some low-lying islands. On this point, see McAdam (2012, pp. 159–160). I return to this point below.

27. A 'decent' life here is merely one where the basic needs of the person in question are met, and the life is normally free of danger and persecution. Some, such as Will Kymlicka, have argued that access to one's own 'societal culture' is necessary for a decent life. See Kymlicka (1996, pp. 75–106). This strikes me as almost certainly false. For argument to that end, see Waldron (1992). The ability of millions of refugees and other migrants to live rich, meaningful lives outside of their original 'societal cultures' tells strongly against Kymlicka's claim, especially in areas relevant to this paper. Even if Kymlicka's claim were more plausible, I would contend that there would be strong pragmatic reasons to avoid extending refugee protection in the way his account might suggest, as the likely outcome would be less protection for those in need, not more.

28. Nothing in the Refugee Convention itself seems to require this, and 'group' designations are sometimes used, at least at first, during mass flight situations. But, most states that accept large number of refugees insist on individualized

determinations, and some, such as the US, require some sort of individualize process before accepting refugees living in camps for resettlement.

29. For helpful discussion, see Price (2009, pp. 174–180) and Gibney (2005).

30. Pre-departure screening and planned, managed, movement is certainly preferable in the first scenario as well, but might be less likely, so I do not want to assume it.

31. By calling this a 'conceptual' question, I do not mean to indicate that it does not have practical implications. Indeed, one part of my argument against 'corporate' remedies will turn on their impracticality, and the adoption of corporate remedies would have many quite serious implications for practice. But, the question is conceptual in the sense that it asks about the nature of our moral duties to certain people, not primarily about procedures or the implementation of them. The papers I consider are, in fact, almost completely silent about how their proposed solutions would be implemented in the real world.

32. Both Nine and Kolers focus on the supposed 'sinking island' case, taken to be one where the entire territory of a state becomes uninhabitable. Other types of movement related to climate change, types we should expect to make up the majority of environmentally related movement, is not seriously considered in either paper, so it is hard to know what remedies, if any, Nine or Kolers would supply in those cases. However, as the cases considered by Nine and Kolers significantly overlaps with the cases where I would extend refugee protection, I will not spend more time on this point.

33. What, exactly, this comes to is a matter of dispute between Nine and Kolers. Nine's view is more literal – territory, in the sense of land, would be transferred from an existing state to the people fleeing the effects of climate change. See Nine (2010, p. 361). Kolers' view is, at least, more complicated, in that he seeks to break the link between territory and land, arguing that 'territory' is a 'normative' term describing 'the ratio of justice to geographical space'. See Kolers (2012, p. 338). This is, at least, a highly idiosyncratic view of territory, and I will admit that I do not think I fully understand it. To my mind, it seems to turn on an implausible metaphor for what plausibility it has, and seems extremely unlikely to be of practical use. At best, Kolers seems to me to be pointing out, in a highly obscure way, that sovereignty over land may be shared by different groups of people. This may be relevant, but putting this in terms of 'creating new territory' or territory being 'positive sum,' as does Kolers, seems to me to obscure the issue rather than clarify it. As much as is possible, I shall try to avoid the dispute between Nine and Kolers on the nature of territory, as I do not think it has significant implications for the view and argument I will present.

34. None of this, of course, is to deny that more corporate responses could not be negotiated. For example, it would not be implausible for the entire (quite small) population of Tuvalu to relocate to New Zealand, as part of a planned movement. But, I shall argue, this would not require granting Tuvaluans special territorial rights in New Zealand.

35. A 'primary rights' account to self-determination and secession is one that does not base the exercise of the right on any prior wrongdoing by other parties. See Buchanan (2004, p. 353). Examples include Wellman (2005) and Copp (1997).

36. Kolers, as noted, might contest this characterization, given his claim to present a 'normative' notion of territory, where claims are said to not be 'zero sum'. Again, I will note that this seems to me to be little more than a metaphor, and a confused one at best. At the least, control over physical territory will be shared, and so reduced. The examples of Kolers lists, such as shared sovereignty within states, confirm this rather than showing that territory may be non-'zero-sum.'

37. On backlash against refugees in general, see Gibney (2004, pp. 94–103, 177–192).
38. There are many competing accounts of what appropriate minority rights in a liberal state come to. See, in particular, the accounts given by Kymlicka (1996, 2001), Raz (1996), Tan (2002). I make no attempt here to say which is the right account, but any of these is capable of being grafted onto my approach without having to resort to the corporate/territorial view.
39. Of course, one may be morally responsible for harms that are not against an existing law. But, such responsibility does not easily fit within the 'crime' model here under consideration. These harms are, at best, considered under a 'tort' model, though even here foreseeability of harm is significantly relevant for determining moral and legal responsibility. My thanks to an anonymous referee for helpful comments on this point.
40. Of course, a new state could, in some cases, be placed on an existing border, splitting the burden between two or more countries. Or, if we want to allow highly disjoined states, the territory could be even more widely distributed. The first 'solution' seems to me to be unlikely to be of more than minimal help for the real problem here, while the second poses too many problems of practicality. In neither case do these 'solutions' seem to me well calibrated to the actual problems we face. My thanks to an anonymous referee for pointing out the need to say more here.
41. On the need to address this problem, and the difficulties faced, see Lister (forthcoming).

References

Abrar, C., 2005. Bangladesh and India. *In*: M. Gibney and R. Hansen, eds., *Immigration and asylum from 1900 to the present (vol. 3)*. Santa Barbara, CA: ABC-Clio.

Buchanan, A., 2004. *Justice, legitimacy, and self-determination: moral foundations for international law*. Oxford: Oxford University Press.

Chang, H., 2010. The environment and climate change: is international migration part of the problem or part of the solution? *Fordham environmental law review*, 20, 341–356.

Copp, D., 1997. Democracy and communal self-determination. *In*: R. McKim and J. McMahan, eds., *The morality of nationalism*. Oxford: Oxford University Press.

Crepeau, F., et al., 2006. *Forced migration and global process: a view from forced migration studies*. Lanham, MD: Lexington Books.

Gibney, M., 2004. *The ethics and politics of asylum*. Cambridge: Cambridge University Press.

Gibney, M., 2005. Temporary protection. *In*: M. Gibney and R. Hansen eds., *Immigration and asylum: from 1900 to the present (vol. 3)*. Santa Barbara: ABC-Clio.

Gibney, M. and Hansen, R., eds., 2005. *Immigration and asylum: from 1900 to the present (vol. 3)*. Santa Barbara: ABC-Clio.

Goodwin-Gill, G., 1998. *The refugee in international law*. 2nd ed. Oxford: Oxford University Press.

Hosein, A., unpublished. The fundamental argument for legalization.

Kolers, A., 2012. Floating provisos and sinking islands. *Journal of applied philosophy*, 29, 333–343.

Kymlicka, W., 1996. *Multicultural citizenship*. Oxford: Oxford University Press.

Kymlicka, W., 2001. *Politics in the vernacular*. Oxford: Oxford University Press.

Lister, M., forthcoming. Self-determination, dissent, and the problem of population transfers. *In*: F. Teson, ed. *The problem of self-determination*. Cambridge: Cambridge University Press.

Lister, M., 2013. Who are refugees? *Law and philosophy*, 32, 645–671.

McAdam, J., 2012. *Climate change, forced migration, and international law*. Oxford: Oxford University Press.

Musalo, K., 1994. Irreconcilable differences? Divorcing refugee protection from human rights norms. *Michigan journal of international law*, 15, 1179–1240.

National Public Radio, 2013. *Impossible choice faces America's first 'climate refugees'*. Available from: http://www.npr.org/2013/05/18/185068648/impossible-choice-faces-americas-first-climate-refugees [Accessed 4 July 2013].

Nine, C., 2010. Ecological refugees, states borders, and the lockean proviso. *Journal of applied philosophy*, 27, 359–375.

Plumer, B., 2012. What we know about climate change and drought. *The Washington post*. Available from: http://www.washingtonpost.com/blogs/wonkblog/wp/2012/07/24/what-we-know-about-climate-change-and-drought/ [Accessed 4 July 2013].

Price, M., 2009. *Rethinking asylum*. Cambridge: Cambridge University Press.

Rawls, J., 1996. *Political Liberalism*. (Paperback ed.). New York, NY: Columbia University Press.

Rawls, J., 1999. *The law of peoples: with "the idea of public reason revisited"*. Cambridge, MA: Harvard University Press.

Raz, J., 1996. *Ethics in the public domain: essays in the morality of law and politics*. Oxford: Oxford University Press.

Risse, M., 2009. The right to relocation: disappearing island nations and common ownership of the earth. *Ethics & international affairs*, 23 (3), 281–300.

Tan, K.C., 2002. *Toleration, diversity, and global justice*. University Park, PA: Pennsylvania State University Press.

Waldron, J., 1992. Minority cultures and the cosmopolitan alternative. *University of Michigan journal of law reform*, 25, 751–793.

Wellman, C.H., 2005. *A theory of secession: the case for political self-determination*. Cambridge: Cambridge University Press.

Index

Note: 'n' after a page number indicates a note.

redistribution of wealth. *See* wealth
   redistribution
refugees: from climate change 62, 126–37;
   definition of 8, 62; detention 116; and
   individualized protection 133–6; limits
   to asylum for 129–33; and moral
   obligation to admit 62–3; UN definition
   of 126, 128–9; from war 62. *See also*
   asylum; immigrants
remedial rights approach 135–6
rights: Rawls on political 94; of
   undocumented immigrants 58–9
Risse, M. 132, 136

safety zones 109, 118–19, 120
Sager, Alex 5, 8, 94
Sassen, Saskia 83
Scheffler, Samuel: on cultural identity
   17–18; on national identity 18–19
Schmidt, V. 98
'sedentary bias' 75
self-determination 134–5
Shachar, A. 115
Silverman, Stephanie 7
'sinking island' case 140n32
social cohesion 3
social justice policies 3
social services: and legal residents 55; and
   temporary workers 57
sovereignty 3; Miller on 117–18; and
   morality of immigration 47–8; vs. open
   borders 116; power of exclusion in 62–3
Soysal, Yasmin 22
states, obligations of human rights on
   39–40
Stivers, Herbert 32

taxation 77–8
temporal issues: Carens on 6; and
   detention 110–11, 113, 119; of
   immigration 5–7, 48, 51, 59
temporary migrants 56–7; behaviour of 91;
   and citizenship 92; demographics of 90;
   inclusion of 88–9; organizations

advocating for 97–100; vs. other
   marginalised groups 95–6; trapped in
   host countries 92, 102; and voting rights
   93–7; vulnerability of 91–2, 93–4
temporary migration programs 103n1
temporary migration projects: definition of
   89–90; effect of, on democratic
   institutions 100–2; in European Union
   90
Tesón, Fernando 71
Thomson, Judith Jarvis 41
Torresi, Tiziana 6
trade unions 6–7, 97, 98–100
transmigrants 74
transnationalism 74

unions. *See* trade unions
United Nations, definition of refugee 126,
   128–9
Universal Declaration of Human Rights
   32
unreason: vs. irrationality 21; role of, and
   immigration 12

Vera Institute of Justice 114
Vezzoli, S. 75
Vietnam War 62
violinist metaphor 41
voting rights 77; vs. citizenship 93, 94; and
   marginalised groups 95–6; and
   temporary migrants 93–7

war 62
warehousing 118
Watson, Lori 24
wealth redistribution: and brain drain 5;
   migration as mechanism for 4–5
Wellman, Christopher Heath 32, 37–8
White Australia Policy 48
Wilcox, S. 110

Young, A. 112, 113
Ypi, Lea 72
Yup'ik Eskimos 131

www.ingramcontent.com/pod-product-compliance
Ingram Content Group UK Ltd.
Pitfield, Milton Keynes, MK11 3LW, UK
UKHW020349010325
455677UK00021B/358